To:

_____

From:

_____

Date:

_____

Copyright © 2007 by Sarah Young

All rights reserved. No portion of this publication may be reproduced,
stored in a retrieval system, or transmitted by any means—electronic,
mechanical, photocopying, recording, or any other—except for brief quotations
in printed reviews, without the prior written permission of the publisher.

Published in Nashville, Tennessee, by Thomas Nelson, Inc.

Unless otherwise indicated, Scripture quotations are taken from the
New International Version © 1984 by the International Bible Society.
Used by permission of Zondervan Bible Publishers.

Other Scripture quotations are taken from the *New American Standard Bible* (NASB)
© 1960, 1962, 1963, 1971, 1972, 1973, 1975, and 1977 by the Lockman Foundation.
Used by permission. (www.Lockman.org); *Amplified® Bible* (AMP) © 1954, 1958, 1962,
1964, 1965, 1987 by The Lockman Foundation. Used by permission. (www.Lockman.org);
New King James Version (NKJV) ©1979, 1980, 1982, 1992, Thomas Nelson, Inc.

Project Developer: Lisa Stilwell
Project Editor: Steffany Woolsey Creative Services, Inc.
Designed by ThinkPen Design

ISBN-10: 1-4041-0495-X
ISBN-13: 978-1-4041-0495-2

Printed and bound in China
www.thomasnelson.com

Seeking His Light *in* Your Life

Dear Jesus

Sarah Young

AUTHOR OF *Jesus Calling*

THOMAS NELSON
Since 1798

NASHVILLE   DALLAS   MEXICO CITY   RIO DE JANEIRO   BEIJING

Dedication

To Jesus,
the Light of the world,
who called me out
of darkness into
His marvelous Light—
that I may proclaim
His excellencies!

Introduction

Dear Jesus emerged from my personal struggles—
with circumstances, with people, and with God. Over
the years I have contended with numerous health
problems and surgeries. I've lived in many situations
and places where my strengths were largely irrelevant
and my weaknesses were all too evident. Had my life
been easier, I could not have written this book.

Most of the first decade of my marriage was spent
in Japan, where I was truly a "square peg in a round
hole." Stripped of my cultural props, I discovered
a vast neediness within me. I also came to realize
that *people* were insufficient to meet all those needs.
Already a Christian, I finally turned wholeheartedly
to my living Lord. I sought to know Him more
intimately, to become increasingly aware of His
continual Presence.

My first devotional book, *Jesus Calling*, grew
out of writings gleaned from my times of focused
concentration on Jesus: waiting in His Presence,
listening in my mind for His communications. As I
listened and wrote, I continually asked for the Holy
Spirit's help.

Several years after I began this listening adventure, I organized some of the writings into daily readings. My arrangement of most of the readings seemed somewhat random, but readers of *Jesus Calling* have told me countless times that writings assigned to specific days of the year spoke precisely to their needs and circumstances on those days.

Eventually, I realized that *God* had orchestrated all those details: accomplishing His vast purposes in ways that display His infinite intelligence. As I ponder His unfathomable ways, my heart resonates with the apostle Paul's words: "Oh, the depth of the riches of the wisdom and knowledge of God! How unsearchable his judgments, and his paths beyond tracing out" (Romans 11:33).

I wrote *Dear Jesus* in the same listening-to-God mode that I used with *Jesus Calling*. I've continued to write with the help of Christ's Spirit, who guides my thinking while I listen in His Presence. I believe the Bible is the only infallible Word of God. My writings are based on that absolute standard, and I try to ensure they are consistent with Scripture.

The devotions in *Dear Jesus* are structured in a dialogue format. Each entry has three sections: The first and third parts, which are printed in gold, are written from the perspective of Jesus speaking; the second section is my personal response. It is genuine—expressing actual struggles and longings. Yet it represents not only me but also others who seek growing intimacy with Christ. Since you are reading this book, I assume you are among these seekers.

The dialogue format is designed to help you go deeper in your relationship with Jesus—bringing more and more aspects of your life to Him. When I journal, I often find it helpful to pour out my heart to God before waiting quietly in His Presence. Having unburdened myself, I am better able to hear Him. Also, my listening is more focused when I bring specific concerns to Him.

I trust that the issues I address in *Dear Jesus* are matters close to your heart as well. I included a topical index with this book, to help guide you to readings that are especially relevant to your current circumstances and struggles.

Most of the devotions in *Dear Jesus* begin with brief passages from *Jesus Calling*. I chose thought-provoking portions that invite you to dive in, searching for hidden treasure. Some of the devotions begin with selections from the Bible or from my previously unpublished writing. Each daily reading is followed by a few Scripture references which are written out for you.

I want you to know how important each reader is to me. I pray daily for everyone who is reading *Jesus Calling*, and now that *Dear Jesus* is published, I will also pray for readers of this book.

My ardent desire is that our Lord will use *Dear Jesus* powerfully in your life—drawing you ever nearer, blessing you with joyful awareness of His Presence.

Sarah Young

"I am the
light of the world.
Whoever follows me
will never walk in darkness,
but will have the
light of life."

JOHN 8:12

> I, the Lover of your soul, understand you
> perfectly and love you eternally.

Dear Jesus,

I'm thankful it is my soul You love, rather than my appearance or performance. So often, I'm dissatisfied with both of these, especially when I make them my focus. I'm grateful for Your perfect understanding, since I sometimes feel misunderstood or simply overlooked. Help me experience more fully Your compassionate, unfailing Love.

Beloved, relax in My loving Presence. Let the Light of My Love soak into your entire being. Rest deeply while I massage your thoughts and feelings, helping you change focus from yourself to Me. *Cease striving and know that I am God.* I created you to know Me: to enjoy Me and center your life in Me.

The world abounds with idols—things you turn to when you want to feel better about yourself: eating, entertainment, exercise, mastery of something or someone. However, none of these things can slake the thirst of your soul, which yearns for Me alone. Idolatrous substitutes may suppress your appetite for Me, mainly by distracting you, but they provide no satisfaction. When you get that gnawing sensation around the edges of your soul, return to Me. Your soul will be satisfied as with the richest of foods.

"Though the mountains be shaken and the hills be removed, yet my unfailing love for you will not be shaken nor my covenant of peace be removed," says the LORD, who has compassion on you.
Isaiah 54:10

Cease striving and know that I am God;
I will be exalted among the nations,
I will be exalted in the earth.
Psalm 46:10 NASB

O God, you are my God, earnestly I seek you;
my soul thirsts for you...
I have seen you in the sanctuary
and beheld your power and your glory.
Because your love is better than life,
my lips will glorify you.
I will praise you as long as I live,
and in your name I will lift up my hands.
My soul will be satisfied as with the richest of foods;
with singing lips my mouth will praise you.
Psalm 63:1–5

> Each moment you can choose
> to practice My Presence or to practice
> the presence of problems.

Dear Jesus,

You know how I long to practice Your Presence more consistently. When I keep my focus on You, my whole perspective is brighter, more joyful. When I'm preoccupied with problems, I feel weighed down and anxious. Yet the default setting of my mind seems to be problem-solving. My thoughts tend to flow toward finding what is wrong and trying to fix it. I want to break free from this hurtful pattern, but its roots go deep into my being.

Beloved, come to Me and rest in My sufficiency. Stop trying to fix yourself by focusing on your failures. Remember that the world you inhabit is fallen, and you are part of that brokenness. You can no more practice My Presence perfectly than you can save yourself from your sins. In a fallen world, all your default settings are tainted by sin. Nonetheless, you are being transformed and renewed by My Spirit within you.

Collaborate with Me as I work to set you free from hurtful ways. View each moment as a fresh opportunity to draw near Me. I welcome you with open arms.

Come to Me, all you who are weary
and burdened, and I will give you rest.
Matthew 11:28

Do not conform any longer to the pattern of this world,
but be transformed by the renewing of your mind.
Then you will be able to test and approve what
God's will is—his good, pleasing and perfect will.
Romans 12:2

Search me, O God, and know my heart;
Try me and know my anxious thoughts;
And see if there be any hurtful way in me,
And lead me in the everlasting way.
Psalm 139:23–24 NASB

> I am training you to hold in your heart a dual focus: My continual Presence and the hope of heaven.

Dear Jesus,

There is no deeper comfort than knowing in my heart that You are with me always: here on earth and throughout eternity in heaven. I have known this great truth in my head for many years. However, my heart is fickle and tends to chase after other gods. Only as Your Spirit helps me can I grasp the awesomeness of Your Presence with me forever.

Beloved, trust Me to do in you what you could never do for yourself. I am indeed with you—watching over you wherever you are, wherever you go. Simply accept My Presence with you as reality: the deepest Reality. Build your life on this absolute truth, which is like building your house on a rock.

Your heart and mind *will* wander away from Me, but My Spirit within can remind you to return. Ask the Holy Spirit to help you in this way. He delights in being your Helper.

Rejoice that I am with you not only in this life but also in the life to come. Let the promise of heaven flood your heart with My eternal Presence!

I am with you and will watch over you wherever you go,
and I will bring you back to this land. I will not leave you
until I have done what I have promised you.
Genesis 28:15

Therefore everyone who hears these words
of mine and puts them into practice is like
a wise man who built his house on the rock.
Matthew 7:24

I will ask the Father, and He will give you another Helper,
that He may be with you forever; that is the Spirit of truth,
whom the world cannot receive, because it does not see
Him or know Him, but you know Him because He abides
with you and will be in you.
John 14:16–17 NASB

In my Father's house are many rooms; if it were not so,
I would have told you. I am going there to prepare a place for you.
And if I go and prepare a place for you, I will come back
and take you to be with me that you also may be where I am.
John 14:2–3

> Do not fear your weakness, for it is the stage on which My Power and My Glory perform most brilliantly.

Dear Jesus,

I want to be available for the display of Your Power and Glory. But I feel more like a splintery, unfinished platform than a polished, ready-to-use stage. I may not even be safe enough for Your performance, since some of my boards aren't nailed down properly.

Beloved, no matter how polished you might become, you could never be good enough for the display of My radiant holiness. However, I have chosen you to reflect My Glory, despite your imperfections. Moreover, your weakness is the ideal stage for the exhibition of My Power. Your part in this drama is to look away from yourself and gaze at Me in My awesome splendor. Forget about your unworthiness and delight yourself in My glorious Being. Watch while I perform great things for you.

But he said to me, "My grace is sufficient for you,
for my power is made perfect in weakness."
Therefore I will boast all the more gladly about my
weaknesses, so that Christ's power may rest on me.

2 Corinthians 12:9

And we, who with unveiled faces all reflect the Lord's glory,
are being transformed into his likeness with ever-increasing glory,
which comes from the Lord, who is the Spirit.

2 Corinthians 3:18

Who among the gods is like you, O LORD?
Who is like you—majestic in holiness,
awesome in glory, working wonders?

Exodus 15:11

Delight yourself in the LORD and he
will give you the desires of your heart.

Psalm 37:4

> I am the firm Foundation on which you can dance and sing and celebrate My Presence.

Dear Jesus,

I long to dance for You, sing praises to You, and celebrate Your Presence continually. However, most of the time I feel earthbound and weighed down. Worshiping you requires the engagement of my entire being—something I delight in and yet somehow resist. Teach me how to celebrate You more consistently, more abundantly.

Beloved, begin by lingering in My peaceful Presence. As you relax in My everlasting arms, sense how safe and secure you are. I am indeed the rock-solid Foundation on which you can live exuberantly. Dancing, singing, and praying are ways you can express your delight in Me.

My very Presence radiates Joy in vast, unmeasured fullness! When you praise Me, your Joy increases, as does your awareness of My holy Presence. Your body may or may not be mightily engaged in this endeavor, but I see into your heart. That is where the ultimate celebration of My Presence takes place.

The eternal God is your refuge,
and underneath are the everlasting arms.
Deuteronomy 33:27

You have made known to me the path of life;
you will fill me with joy in your presence,
with eternal pleasures at your right hand.
Psalm 16:11

David, wearing a linen ephod,
danced before the LORD with all his might.
2 Samuel 6:14

But the LORD said to Samuel, "Do not look at his appearance
or at his physical stature, because I have refused him.
For the LORD does not see as man sees; for man looks
at the outward appearance, but the LORD looks at the heart.
1 Samuel 16:7 NKJV

> Every time you thank Me, you acknowledge
> that I am your Lord and Provider.
> This is the proper stance for a child
> of God: receiving with thanksgiving.

Dear Jesus,

I know I'm supposed to give thanks in all circumstances. But sometimes my words ring hollow: I can say them without feeling the least bit thankful. It's especially hard for me to be thankful in the midst of a bad day, when everything seems to be going wrong.

Beloved, I know what goes on in your heart far better than you do. I know when you feel thankful, and when you don't. However, I can also see in the depths of your heart a desire to please Me by offering thanks even when you don't feel like it.

When you struggle to be thankful, stop and remember who I Am: the Author of your life and your faith. You are utterly dependent on Me for everything, including your next breath. Every good gift is from Me!

When you thank Me during a difficult day, you are assuming the proper stance for a child of God. If you persevere in this thankfulness, resisting the temptation to grumble, you can find Joy and Peace in the midst of your struggles.

Give thanks in all circumstances,
for this is God's will for you in Christ Jesus.
1 Thessalonians 5:18

You killed the author of life, but God raised him
from the dead. We are witnesses of this.
Acts 3:15

Every good and perfect gift is from above,
coming down from the Father of the heavenly lights,
who does not change like shifting shadows.
James 1:17

Therefore, since we are receiving a kingdom
that cannot be shaken, let us be thankful, and so
worship God acceptably with reverence and awe.
Hebrews 12:28

> Miracles are not always visible to the naked eye, but those who live by faith can see them clearly. Living by faith, rather than sight, enables you to see My Glory.

Dear Jesus,

I want to see Your Glory! Please give me discerning eyes, so I can recognize miracles when I see them. Help me to be increasingly aware of You—living by faith, not by sight.

Beloved, come into the radiance of My Love-Light. Let My healing Presence nourish and renew you. Be content with a simple, quiet life. Instead of shaking the bushes—trying to make things happen—wait to see what I am doing. I am at work in many areas of your life long before you can discern results. Trust Me by waiting patiently, accepting each moment as a gift from Me. When time is right, you will see the results of My handiwork. You may even get a glimpse of My Glory. Don't try to hold on to Glory-moments. Simply enjoy them gratefully; then release them back to Me.

Anticipate living with Me in heaven, where My Glory will be your continual experience: lighting up your life forever. Look forward to the radiant perfection awaiting you, but remember that the world you now inhabit is deeply fallen. Living by faith enables you to accept this world's brokenness, yet remain open to seeing My glorious miracles.

Then Jesus said, "Did I not tell you that if you believed, you would see the glory of God?"
John 11:40

We live by faith, not by sight.
2 Corinthians 5:7

I wait for you, O LORD;
you will answer, O LORD my God.
Psalm 38:15

The city does not need the sun or the moon to shine on it, for the glory of God gives it light, and the Lamb is its lamp.
Revelation 21:23

> An ongoing problem is like a tutor who is always by your side. The learning possibilities are limited only by your willingness to be teachable.

Dear Jesus,

I confess that I don't like this tutor at all! What I really want is to break free and run away from my problems. Haven't I spent enough time with this teacher? Surely there must be other ways I could learn.

Beloved, I don't expect you to like your tutor. No one enjoys having problems. However, I do require you to accept your tutor's presence with you as long as I choose. The bottom line is whether you trust Me to use the difficulty for good in your life. Beware of feeling entitled to an easy life. I actually promised the opposite when I said, "In this world you will have trouble." If you want to learn all that I have prepared for you, you must accept My teaching methods. Remember that I am the Potter, and you are the clay. You need to be flexible—malleable in My skillful hands.

Try to see your problem as a disguised blessing, gradually transforming you into My likeness. When you accept My ways with you trustingly—without rebelling or running away—you find freedom through My Spirit. Even more wondrously, I empower you to reflect Me to others with ever-increasing Glory!

I have told you these things, so that in me you
may have peace. In this world you will have trouble.
But take heart! I have overcome the world.
John 16:33

Yet, O LORD, you are our Father.
We are the clay, you are the potter;
we are all the work of your hand.
Isaiah 64:8

Now the Lord is the Spirit, and where the Spirit of the Lord is,
there is freedom. And we, who with unveiled faces all reflect the
Lord's glory, are being transformed into his likeness with
ever-increasing glory, which comes from the Lord, who is the Spirit.
2 Corinthians 3:17–18

> A successful day is one in which you have
> stayed in touch with Me, even if many
> things remain undone at the end of the day.

Dear Jesus,

That sounds almost too good to be true. I rarely
reach the end of the day feeling successful. I nearly
always experience a sense of some degree of failure.
There are numerous ways of measuring success, and
I feel the pull of many of them. That can leave me in
a fragmented, unfocused condition. Help me to view
success from Your perspective.

Beloved, there are indeed many measures of
success in the world, and most of them are
meaningless. To avoid confusion, you need a rule of
thumb: Seek to please Me. When communicating
with Me is your highest priority, I am pleased. The
more you commune with Me as you go through a
day, the more you walk in My ways. The Light of
My Presence illumines the path before you, making

sin both obvious and abhorrent. This same Light satisfies your soul. So, staying in touch with Me is an excellent measure of success.

Jesus replied: "'Love the Lord your God with all your heart and with all your soul and with all your mind.' This is the first and greatest commandment."
Matthew 22:37–38

You have set our iniquities before you, our secret sins in the light of your presence.
Psalm 90:8

This is what the LORD says: "Stand at the crossroads and look; ask for the ancient paths, ask where the good way is, and walk in it, and you will find rest for your souls."
Jeremiah 6:16

My soul shall be satisfied as with marrow and fatness, And my mouth shall praise You with joyful lips.
Psalm 63:5 NKJV

> Trust in Me with all your heart and mind,
> and do not lean on your own understand-
> ing. In all your ways acknowledge Me,
> and I will make your path straight.

Dear Jesus,

Trusting You with all my heart has been my goal for years, but I seem to be making little progress. I suspect the culprit is my mind's ravenous appetite for understanding. Behind this impetus to understand, there lies strong desire to feel in control of my life. I want to trust You wholeheartedly, but I feel stuck.

Beloved, your desire to trust Me wholeheartedly is a worthy goal, and it is pleasing to Me. I am providing training through your life experiences. Allow Me to do this supernatural work in your heart. Recognize that many of the difficulties in your life are designed to help in this endeavor.

I want you to trust Me with all your heart *and* all your mind. The Holy Spirit will help you think trusting thoughts, but He requires your cooperation.

Instead of relying on your own understanding to help you feel in control, ask My Spirit to control your mind. Then, wait confidently to see results. As you look to Me, trusting Me and talking with Me, I straighten out the path before you.

Lean on, trust in, and be confident in the Lord with all your heart and mind and do not rely on your own insight or understanding. In all your ways know, recognize, and acknowledge Him, and He will direct and make straight and plain your paths.
Proverbs 3:5–6 AMP

Commit your way to the LORD, trust also in Him, and He shall bring it to pass.
Psalm 37:5 NKJV

The mind of sinful man is death, but the mind controlled by the Spirit is life and peace.
Romans 8:6

> Do not seek approval in the mirror
> or in the eyes of other people.
> In My Presence you have infinite approval.

Dear Jesus,

It's so easy for me to judge myself on the basis of what I see in the mirror. I know that is fickle and shallow, because my mirror-image is always changing. I'm equally enslaved to viewing myself through the eyes of other people. I tend to evaluate my interpersonal performance rigorously, and I am almost always displeased with something I have said or done. I desperately desire to experience Your approval!

Beloved, "enslaved" is an appropriate word to use. You are indeed a slave when you try to see and judge yourself through people's eyes. Evaluating your worth on the basis of how you look, to yourself or to others, is always a trap. It's as if you are sifting sand, searching for gold—yet looking only at the grains of sand filtering through the sieve, ignoring the gold nuggets that remain. The gold represents the eternal part of you: your soul.

It is invisible to everyone but Me, the One who plans to spend eternity with you. Though invisible, a well-nurtured soul can actually improve your appearance: As you rest in the certainty of My unfailing Love, your face glows with the Joy of My Presence.

My approval of you is infinite because it will continue forever. It is based entirely on My righteousness, which is yours for all eternity. When you look in a mirror, try to see yourself as you truly are—arrayed in perfect righteousness, adorned in glowing approval.

Satisfy us in the morning with your unfailing love,
that we may sing for joy and be glad all our days.
Psalm 90:14

Surely you have granted him eternal blessings
and made him glad with the joy of your presence.
Psalm 21:6

I delight greatly in the LORD; my soul rejoices in my God.
For he has clothed me with garments of salvation and
arrayed me in a robe of righteousness, as a bridegroom
adorns his head like a priest, and as a bride adorns
herself with her jewels.
Isaiah 61:10

Do not feel guilty about taking time to be still in My Presence. You are simply responding to the tugs of divinity within you. I made you in My image, and I hid heaven in your heart.

Dear Jesus,

Being still in Your Presence is quite a challenge, partly because I have to fend off guilt feelings. It seems somehow selfish to spend so much time seeking Your Face. However, at a deeper level, it seems like the most important thing I do.

I yearn for more than this world can provide. I know heaven will satisfy all those longings perfectly. Yet my seeking heart looks to You even now for a taste of that eternal reality.

Beloved, you were not designed to find total satisfaction in this world, because you were crafted in My image. Heaven is your ultimate home, and I placed a bit of heavenly matter in your heart so you would seek Me. I delight in your seeking heart.

Refuse to feel guilty about something that brings Me such pleasure!

Much of this world's angst is actually a longing for the perfection of heaven. Blatant sin is often a misguided attempt to fill that emptiness. The god of this age has blinded the minds of unbelievers, so they search for heaven in hellish ways: excesses and perversions of every kind. However, great sinners can be transformed into exceptional Christians when they turn their passionate appetites toward Me. My Love and forgiveness satisfy soul-hunger as nothing else can.

Look to the LORD and his strength; seek his face always.
Psalm 105:4

The god of this age has blinded the minds of unbelievers,
so that they cannot see the light of the gospel of the
glory of Christ, who is the image of God.
2 Corinthians 4:4

Why spend money on what is not bread, and your labor
on what does not satisfy? Listen, listen to me and eat
what is good, and your soul will delight in the richest of fare.
Isaiah 55:2

> Instead of striving for a predictable, safe lifestyle, seek to know Me in greater depth and breadth. I want to make your life a glorious adventure, but you must stop clinging to old ways.

Dear Jesus,

You know how ambivalent my heart is. I long for the glorious adventure that a life abandoned to You can be. At the same time I cling to old ways, because change frightens me. I feel safest when my life is predictable and things seem to be under control. Help me break free and discover the adventures You have planned for me.

Beloved, the greatest adventure is knowing Me superabundantly: discovering how wide and long and high and deep is My Love for you. The power of My vast Love can feel overwhelming. That is why many people choose to limit their knowledge of Me, keeping Me at a safe distance. How that grieves Me! People settle for mediocrity because it feels more comfortable. However, they continue to battle fear. Only My Love is strong enough to break the hold that fear has on you. A predictable lifestyle may feel safer, but it can shield you from what you need most of all—Me!

When unexpected events shake up your routines, rejoice. This is exactly what you need, to wake you up and point you toward Me. Recognize that you are on the threshold of a new adventure, and that I will be with you every step of the way. As we venture out together, cling tightly to My hand. The more you abandon yourself to Me, the more exuberantly you can experience My Love.

And I pray that you, being rooted and established in love,
may have power, together with all the saints, to grasp
how wide and long and high and deep is the love of Christ.
Ephesians 3:17–18

There is no fear in love. But perfect love drives out fear,
because fear has to do with punishment.
The one who fears is not made perfect in love.
1 John 4:18

My soul clings to you; your right hand upholds me.
Psalm 63:8

Accept each day just as it comes to you.
Do not waste your time and energy wishing
for a different set of circumstances.
Instead, trust Me enough to yield
to My design and purposes.

Dear Jesus,

I waste so much time and energy yearning for
different circumstances. When it's cold, I long for
warmer weather. When it's hot, I look forward to the
crisp coolness of autumn. This is illustrative of how
my mind works: rejecting the day's circumstances and
daydreaming about how I would like things to be. I
realize this is arrogant and foolish, but my mind—left
to itself—tends to work that way. I really want to accept
each day just as it comes to me, but I seem to have little
control over my thoughts.

Beloved, you are right in recognizing that you need
more control over your thinking. Human minds,
though capable of brilliance, tend to be undisciplined
and rebellious. To counteract this weakness, I have

provided help in the Person of the Holy Spirit. As you allow Him, He will control your mind. He offers Life and Peace to those who yield themselves to Him.

Your time and energy are limited; only I know how much of each you have. Try to accept each day as a precious gift from Me, thanking Me for it rather than wishing it away. Ask Me to accomplish My purposes in and through you this day. Instead of wasting so much energy longing for what is not, invest that energy in trusting Me. Daydreaming will leave you empty and discontent, whereas trusting will draw you into My joyful Presence. As you come close to Me, I embrace you in My everlasting arms.

Those who live according to the sinful nature have their
minds set on what that nature desires; but those who
live in accordance with the Spirit have their minds set on
what the Spirit desires. The mind of sinful man is death,
but the mind controlled by the Spirit is life and peace.
Romans 8:5–6

And we know that in all things God works for the good of those
who love him, who have been called according to his purpose.
Romans 8:28

This is the day the LORD has made; let us rejoice and be glad in it.
Psalm 118:24

> To receive My Peace, you must change your grasping, controlling stance to one of openness and trust. The only thing you can grasp without damaging your soul is My hand.

Dear Jesus,

Grasping and controlling are ways I try to feel safe. However, I've come to realize they are hurtful ways that are actually counterproductive. The more I manipulate and grasp for control, the more anxious I become. Even if I succeed through these means, I know the success may be only temporary. Since I am the one who made things happen, I have to patrol the situation vigilantly—or risk losing the ground I've gained. Help me open my grasping hands to You, Lord, trustfully receiving all that You have for me.

Beloved, what you do with your body can help or hinder what goes on in your soul. When you realize you are grasping for control, become aware of your body language. Intentionally open your hands, releasing the matter to Me and inviting Me to take charge. Open your heart and mind also, as you lift your hands to Me. You are now in a good position to receive many blessings from Me, not the least of which is awareness of My Presence. Enjoy the Peace that flows out from Me, while you bask in the Light of My Love. When you move back into your activities, consciously grasp My hand in childlike dependence. For I am the Lord your God, who takes hold of your right hand and says to you, "Do not fear; I will help you."

I want men everywhere to lift up holy hands in prayer,
without anger or disputing.
1 Timothy 2:8

On the evening of that first day of the week,
when the disciples were together,
with the doors locked for fear of the Jews,
Jesus came and stood among them and said,
"Peace be with you!"
John 20:19

Therefore whoever humbles himself as this
little child is the greatest in the kingdom of heaven.
Matthew 18:4, NKJV

For I am the LORD, your God,
who takes hold of your right hand and says to you,
Do not fear; I will help you.
Isaiah 41:13

In a world of unrelenting change,
I am the One who never changes.
I am the Alpha and the Omega, the
Beginning and the End. Find in Me the
stability for which you have yearned.

Dear Jesus,

Sometimes my head spins with all the changes going on in the world around me. The more I focus on them, the more unsteady I feel. I long for stability, for permanence of some sort, but the world provides only ever-increasing rates of change. So I look to You, to provide what this world cannot.

Beloved, your yearning for permanence is good, because it is a longing for eternal, invisible reality. That reality is primarily about Me, and I draw near in response to your seeking heart. I am able to give you a firm place to stand, setting your feet on a rock. You may wonder where such a place can be found. It also is invisible. I am your Rock, your Fortress, your Stronghold. Take refuge in Me, and you will find Me sufficient.

He said to me: "It is done. I am the Alpha and
the Omega, the Beginning and the End.
To him who is thirsty I will give to drink without
cost from the spring of the water of life."
Revelation 21:6

Now to the King eternal, immortal, invisible, the only God,
be honor and glory for ever and ever. Amen.
1 Timothy 1:17

He lifted me out of the slimy pit,
out of the mud and mire;
he set my feet on a rock
and give me a firm place to stand.
Psalm 40:2

The LORD is my rock, my fortress and my deliverer;
my God is my rock, in whom I take refuge.
He is my shield and the horn of
my salvation, my stronghold.
Psalm 18:2

> My kingdom is not about earning and deserving; it is about believing and receiving.

Dear Jesus,

That is very good news, because I could never work hard enough or be good enough to deserve Your kingdom. Yet I struggle with a strong desire to earn my way—at least partially—rather than simply receive everything from You. In some ways, believing and receiving seem more difficult than earning and deserving. I find myself wanting recognition for my efforts and accomplishments. Help me to desire Your way more than mine.

Beloved, I know how vulnerable you are to idolatry. One of the most prevalent temptations is to idolize yourself or your own good works. For this reason, I often withhold success until people are weak enough to handle it. When they have been sufficiently broken by adversity and failure, they are better able to deal with success. So, when trials of many kinds come your way, receive those things as gifts from Me.

Believe that I know what I am doing and My way is perfect. After you have suffered a little while, I Myself will make you what you ought to be, ground you securely, and strengthen you. This is how I prepare you to share in My eternal Glory.

Consider it pure joy, my brothers,
whenever you face trials of many kinds,
because you know that the testing of your faith
develops perseverance.
James 1:2–3

As for God, his way is perfect;
the word of the LORD is flawless.
He is a shield for all who take refuge in him.
2 Samuel 22:31

And after you have suffered a little while, the God of all grace
[Who imparts all blessing and favor], Who has called you to His
[own] eternal glory in Christ Jesus, will Himself complete and
make you what you ought to be, establish and ground
you securely, and strengthen, and settle you.
1 Peter 5:10 AMP

> Whenever you are tempted to grumble,
> come to Me and talk it out. As you open up
> to Me, I will put My thoughts in your mind
> and My song in your heart.

Dear Jesus,

I am frequently tempted to grumble—more often than I like to admit. There are so many things I would like to be different: in me, in others, in the world. My natural tendency is to brood over these matters, rather than talking them over with you. The longer I focus on these negatives, the more likely I am to grumble. Even when I control what I say out loud, my thoughts tend to be full of complaints. Please help me to think Your thoughts.

Beloved, trust Me by opening up to Me consistently. Don't wait till you're already discouraged to bring Me your concerns. As we talk about these matters, remember to thank Me. In spite of how you're feeling, you can thank Me for listening and caring; also, for loving you sufficiently to die for you. Your thankfulness will provide a helpful framework for viewing the things that concern you. Talk about these concerns with Me. Let the Light of My Face shine upon you, as we discuss these matters. Eventually, this heavenly Light will break through the fog in your mind, enabling you to see things from My perspective.

Your communion with Me will bless you in another way also: You will find in My Presence irrepressible Joy. Whether or not I change your circumstances, you will discover I have put a new song in your heart.

Thanks be to God for his indescribable gift!
2 Corinthians 9:15

The LORD make his face shine upon you and be gracious to you.
Numbers 6:25

You have made known to me the paths of life;
you will fill me with joy in your presence.
Acts 2:28

He put a new song in my mouth, a hymn of praise to our God.
Many will see and fear and put their trust in the LORD.
Psalm 40:3

> My grace is sufficient for you, but its sufficiency is for one day at a time.

Dear Jesus,

I desperately need to learn how to live in the present moment. My mind so easily slips into the future, where worries abound. I also spend way too much time analyzing things in the past. Meanwhile, splendors of the present moment parade before me, and I'm too preoccupied to notice. Part of the problem is my tendency to strive for self-sufficiency. Help me learn to rest in Your sufficiency, depending on You more and more.

Beloved, you need My grace in order to live in the present. Grace is all about My provision for you, and accepting that goes against the grain of your natural tendencies. Do you really believe My grace is sufficient for you? If so, then it makes sense to stop your anxious striving.

My grace is indeed sufficient for every situation you will ever encounter. However, you must learn to receive My provisions by looking to Me continually.

Each day you face a number of situations requiring My help. Moment by moment, I proffer to you the needed assistance. Your part is to recognize your neediness and receive what I offer. My Presence is with you always, providing everything you need. Don't worry about tomorrow's needs. My sufficiency is for one day at a time—today!

But he said to me, "My grace is sufficient for you,
for my power is made perfect in weakness." Therefore
I will boast all the more gladly about my weaknesses,
so that Christ's power may rest on me.
2 Corinthians 12:9

Those who look to him are radiant;
their faces are never covered with shame.
Psalm 34:5

And my God will meet all your needs according
to his glorious riches in Christ Jesus.
Philippians 4:19

Therefore do not worry about tomorrow,
for tomorrow will worry about itself.
Each day has enough trouble of its own.
Matthew 6:34

> My Power flows most freely into weak
> ones aware of their need for Me.
> Faltering steps of dependence are not lack
> of faith; they are links to My Presence.

Dear Jesus,

My journey is indeed one of faltering steps. Today I feel as if it's a challenge just to take the next step. I find it all too easy to be aware of my neediness. If I didn't know You were with me, I would despair. I confess that I sometimes get discouraged about my ongoing weaknesses. I know that dependence on You brings spiritual blessings, yet at times I feel trapped by my limitations.

Beloved, awareness of your need for Me creates a strong connection to My Presence. My Power flows into you continually: It gives you strength to take the next faltering step, strength to resist discouragement and despair, strength to know Me in intimate dependence. Only My Power can provide such strength, enabling you to live abundantly in the midst of your limitations. Your day-to-day perseverance, in dependence on Me, is every bit as supernatural as an outright miracle.

Because you are My beloved child, I choose to bless you. However, I bless you in ways that are unique to your needs and My design for you. Your difficulties do not signify lack of faith or lack of blessing. They are means to help you stay on the path I have chosen for you. Though the way before you may be steep and rocky, it is nonetheless the path of Life. It is where you encounter My luminous Presence—radiating Peace that transcends your limitations.

Though the fig tree does not bud and there are no grapes on the vines, though the olive crop fails and the fields produce no food, though there are no sheep in the pen and no cattle in the stalls, yet I will rejoice in the LORD, I will be joyful in God my Savior. The sovereign LORD is my strength; he makes my feet like the feet of a deer, he enables me to go on the heights.

Habakkuk 3:17–19

To him who is able to keep you from falling and to present you before his glorious presence without fault and with great joy— to the only God our Savior be glory, majesty, power and authority, through Jesus Christ our Lord, before all ages, now and forevermore! Amen.

Jude 1:24–25

And the peace of God, which transcends all understanding, will guard your hearts and your minds in Christ Jesus.

Philippians 4:7

> Guard your thoughts diligently. Good thought-choices will keep you close to Me.

Dear Jesus,

Sometimes my thoughts seem disconnected from my will. They go off in many directions at once, making it very difficult to focus on one thing. I deeply desire to fix my thoughts on You, Jesus, but it's a constant struggle—like swimming against a strong current.

Beloved, don't be surprised by the fierceness of the battle for your mind. The enemy and his evil army abhor your closeness to Me, so they send missiles of deception into your mind. Fixing your thoughts on Me will continue to be a struggle, because of this ongoing barrage of demonic interference. Another factor is your own fallen nature: Your mind did not escape the effects of the Fall.

Many things can affect your ability to think clearly—poor sleep, health, or nutrition; lack of fresh air and exercise; worries of the world; excessive busyness. Nonetheless, it is still possible to exert much control over your thinking. Ask My Spirit to help you in this endeavor. Don't simply let your thoughts run freely; set a guard over them. Be self-controlled and alert. When you become aware of hurtful or unholy thoughts, bring them to Me. Talk with Me about your struggles; choose to make your thoughts a conversation with Me. As you persevere in making good thought-choices, you will enjoy My refreshing Presence more and more.

Therefore, holy brothers, who share in the
heavenly calling, fix your thoughts on Jesus,
the apostle and high priest whom we confess.
Hebrews 3:1

Set a guard over my mouth, O LORD;
keep watch over the door of my lips.
Psalm 141:3

Be self-controlled and alert. Your enemy the devil prowls
around like a roaring lion looking for someone to devour.
1 Peter 5:8

Repent, then, and turn to God, so that
your sins may be wiped out, that times
of refreshing may come from the Lord.
Acts 3:19

> If you learn to trust Me—really trust Me—
> with your whole being, then nothing can
> separate you from My Peace. Everything
> you endure can be put to good use by
> allowing it to train you in trusting Me.
> This is how you foil the works of evil,
> growing in grace through the very adversity
> that was meant to harm you.

Dear Jesus,

My deepest desire is to trust You with my whole being, but trusting does not come easily to me. I have, however, become more open to accepting adversity as a gift from You. Sometimes I just want relief from my difficulties. At other times I am able to receive them as blessings. Help me to allow my problems to train me in trusting You.

Beloved, it helps to have an eternal perspective. If your life on earth were all there is, it might be reasonable to run from adversity and seek a life of pleasure. However, your earthly lifespan is miniscule, compared with the Glory that awaits you in heaven. A large part of learning to trust Me is viewing your life through this big-picture perspective.

Your openness to accepting adversity as blessing shows that you are indeed learning to trust Me more. Your anticipation of good outcomes in the midst of hard times is a profound form of trust.

Remember that the evil one attacks you continually with burning arrows of accusation. If you use your shield of faith skillfully, you can stop those missiles and extinguish their flames. Even if some of the arrows find their mark and wound you, do not despair. I am the Great Physician: My loving Presence can both heal your wounds and train you to trust Me more. When you are wounded, come close to Me and pay attention to My teaching. As you do so, your faith will be strengthened, enabling you to grow in grace and knowledge of Me—the Lord of Peace.

But as for you, you meant evil against me; but God meant it for good, in order to bring it about as it is this day, to save many people alive.
Genesis 50:20 NKJV

In addition to all this, take up the shield of faith, with which you can extinguish all the flaming arrows of the evil one.
Ephesians 6:16

But grow in the grace and knowledge of our Lord and Savior Jesus Christ. To him be glory both now and forever! Amen.
2 Peter 3:18

> Thank Me when things do not go
> your way, because spiritual blessings
> come wrapped in trials.

Dear Jesus,

If I thank You every time things don't go my way, I'll be thanking You very frequently! Often I feel as if things are stacked against me, seemingly designed to frustrate me. I have to admit that thanking You is one of the last things I feel like doing when I'm frustrated.

Beloved, earth as I originally created it was sublimely perfect. However, the world in its fallen condition is full of frustrations. I understand your feelings, but I still maintain that thanking Me is the best response. When you do so, you acknowledge that I am greater than you and your problems. Thanking Me when you feel like complaining is a supernatural response: It requires the help of My Spirit. As you give thanks in obedience to My Word and in reliance on the Spirit, your feelings of frustration will begin to diminish. Instead of trying harder and harder to make things go your way, you can release your concerns to Me.

Consider the possibility that I may be bringing much good out of the very things that upset you. Open your eyes and your mind, to look for something new. Seek to see things from My perspective, and you will discover treasures in your trials.

> God saw all that he had made,
> and it was very good.
> And there was evening, and there
> was morning—the sixth day.
> *Genesis 1:31*

> Give thanks in all circumstances,
> for this is God's will for you in Christ Jesus.
> *1 Thessalonians 5:18*

> Forget the former things; do not dwell on the past.
> See, I am doing a new thing! Now it springs up;
> do you not perceive it? I am making a way in the desert
> and streams in the wasteland.
> *Isaiah 43:18–19*

> This is the day that I have made! As you rejoice in this day of life, it will yield up to you precious gifts and beneficial training.

Dear Jesus,

Sometimes I find it easy to rejoice and be glad, but this is not one of those times. Today I feel as if I'm climbing uphill on a barren mountain, with bitter winds whipping around me. I know in my mind that You are with me, yet I feel very much alone. This is one of those days when rejoicing seems unattainable. Please help me find all that You have for me in this day.

Beloved, come to Me with all your neediness. Do not despise yourself for feeling joyless. Apart from Me your resources are ever so limited, and adverse circumstances only highlight that insufficiency. Your greatest need is to reconnect with Me at a deep level. You can cry out to Me, "Help me, Jesus!" Then, wait patiently in My Presence. If you are able, sing praise songs to Me. Your weariness will eventually give way to new strength as you trustingly wait upon

Me. With My help you can find precious pleasures I have scattered alongside your path. Moreover, as you persevere in climbing this challenging trail with Me, you reap the benefits of tough training: You discover it is possible to be sorrowful, yet always rejoicing.

> This is the day the LORD has made;
> We will rejoice and be glad in it.
> *Psalm 118:24 NKJV*

> I am the vine; you are the branches.
> If a man remains in me and I in him,
> he will bear much fruit;
> apart from me you can do nothing.
> *John 15:5*

> Though youths grow weary and tired,
> And vigorous young men stumble badly,
> Yet those who wait for the LORD will gain new strength;
> they will mount up with wings like eagles,
> they will run and not get tired
> they will walk and not become weary.
> *Isaiah 40:30–31 NASB*

> Sorrowful, yet always rejoicing;
> poor, yet making many rich;
> having nothing, and yet possessing everything.
> *2 Corinthians 6:10*

I long for you to trust Me enough to be fully
yourself with Me. When you are real with
Me, I am able to bring out the best in you:
the very gifts I have planted in your soul.

Dear Jesus,

Being real with You can be quite painful, because first
I have to be real with myself. It's often easier to ignore
how I'm feeling than to face my misery head-on. When
I'm feeling bad about myself, I would rather numb my
feelings than bring them to You. Give me the courage to
face myself, so I can be real with You.

Beloved,

the best way to face yourself is to remember
you are constantly clothed in My robe of righteousness. I have no illusions about what lies beneath that
pristine garment of salvation. Nonetheless, I take great
delight in you; I even rejoice over you with singing.

Open yourself up to My unfailing Love. Talk with
Me about whatever is bothering you. Experience your
pain in the Light of My loving Presence. In that brilliant
Light you can see your misery more clearly, but do not

despair. Continue looking at your woeful condition, while resting in the assurance of My Love. What you most feared to expose is no match for the Power of My radiant Presence. Entrust yourself into My capable care, asking Me to transform you according to My plans for you. Collaborate with Me as I work on growing the gifts I planted in your soul.

I delight greatly in the LORD; my soul rejoices in my God.
For he has clothed me with garments of salvation and arrayed
me in a robe of righteousness, as a bridegroom adorns his head
like a priest, and as a bride adorns herself with her jewels.
Isaiah 61:10

The LORD your God is with you, he is mighty to save.
He will take great delight in you, he will quiet you with
his love, he will rejoice over you with singing.
Zephaniah 3:17

But I trust in your unfailing love; my heart rejoices in your salvation.
I will sing to the LORD, for he has been good to me.
Psalm 13:5–6

There is no condemnation for those who belong to Me, because through Me the law of the Spirit of Life set you free from the law of sin and death.

Dear Jesus,

I believe You have freed me from condemnation through Your death on the cross for my sins. Yet I continue to struggle with *feelings* of condemnation— sometimes for no apparent reason. I long to experience the full freedom You have made possible. I know I need the help of Your Spirit, but I'm unsure how to engage His assistance.

Beloved, you can ask My Spirit to help you find freedom from condemning feelings. Acknowledge that those feelings have no basis in reality. Then, look to Me through eyes of faith. Delight yourself in My heavenly smile of approval. The more you connect with Me through focusing on My Presence, the more you can receive My loving affirmation. The best antidote to feelings of condemnation is experiencing My Love for you.

You can also fight condemning feelings by pondering the truths of the gospel. The devil is the father of lies, and he specializes in deception. Fight his hellish lies with biblical truth.

Finally, remember that My Spirit is the Spirit of Life. Feelings of condemnation drain you of energy, leaving you vulnerable. As My Spirit fills you with Life, you are empowered to live abundantly—to the full.

Therefore, there is now no condemnation for those
who are in Christ Jesus, because through Christ Jesus the law
of the Spirit of life set me free from the law of sin and death.
Romans 8:1–2

By day the LORD directs his love,
at night his song is with me—
a prayer to the God of my life.
Psalm 42:8

He [the devil] was a murderer from the beginning,
not holding to the truth, for there is no truth in him.
When he lies, he speaks his native language,
for he is a liar and the father of lies.
John 8:44

The thief comes only to steal and destroy;
I have come that they may have life, and have it to the full.
John 10:10

By gazing at Me, you gain My perspective on your life. This time with Me is essential for untangling your thoughts and smoothing out the day before you.

Dear Jesus,

You can easily read my thoughts, and You assess their condition with perfect accuracy. I wake up each morning with thought-fragments racing through my mind. It's hard to untangle my own thinking, because my mental capacity is so limited when I first awake. However, I can look to You, to do for me what I am unable to do for myself.

Beloved, even when your thoughts are scrambled, you can indeed look to Me for help. Many people stumble out of bed in the morning and head straight for the coffee pot. Though they are not yet thinking clearly, they are conscious enough to move toward something that will help untangle their thoughts. I perform a similar function for you, when your mind stumbles in My direction. Ask Me to help you think My thoughts and see things from My perspective. I created you in My image so that you would have this amazing capacity.

As you wait in My Presence, I not only unscramble your thinking, I also straighten your path through the day. I am sovereign over every aspect of your life, so opening up the way before you is no problem for Me. Some people think they don't have time to begin their day with Me. They don't realize how much I can facilitate their activities—removing obstacles, giving insights that save time, and so on. When you spend precious time with Me, I compensate you generously: smoothing out the circumstances of your day.

O LORD, you have searched me and you know me.
You know when I sit and when I rise;
you perceive my thoughts from afar.
Psalm 139:1–2

So God created man in his own image, in the image
of God he created him; male and female he created them.
Genesis 1:27

We wait in hope for the LORD; he is our help and our shield.
In him our hearts rejoice, for we trust in his holy name.
May your unfailing love rest upon us, O LORD,
even as we put our hope in you.
Psalm 33:20–22

Gently bring your attention back to Me, whenever it wanders away. I look for persistence—rather than perfection— in your walk with Me.

Dear Jesus,

It is such a relief to know that You accept my persistence and do not reject me for my many failures. I'm amazed that my mind can wander so far from You very quickly. When I realize this has happened (again!), my natural tendency is to feel discouraged and disappointed with myself. Thank You for accepting me in all my imperfection.

Beloved,

Beloved, I not only accept you as you are, I love you as you are. I died a criminal's death so I could adorn you with My own perfection. That's why bringing your thoughts to Me is so important: It is My perfect righteousness that saves you, and it will never be taken away from you!

You can easily fall prey to self-rejection if you have unrealistic expectations for yourself. I want you to bring your focus back to Me *gently*: without judging yourself. If you express disappointment about your wandering mind, that response will only distract you further. Instead of engaging in such hurtful activity—putting yourself down—persist in returning your attention to Me. I always welcome you back with unfailing Love.

But when this priest had offered for all time one sacrifice for sins, he sat down at the right hand of God. Since that time he waits for his enemies to be made his footstool, because by one sacrifice he has made perfect forever those who are being made holy.
Hebrews 10:12–14

"Martha, Martha," the Lord answered, "you are worried and upset about many things, but only one thing is needed. Mary has chosen what is better, and it will not be taken away from her."
Luke 10:41–42

How priceless is your unfailing love!
Both high and low among men
find refuge in the shadow of your wings.
Psalm 36:7

> Nothing is wasted when it is shared with Me. I can bring beauty out of the ashes of lost dreams. I can glean Joy out of sorrow, Peace out of adversity. Only a Friend who is also the King of kings could accomplish this divine alchemy.

Dear Jesus,

I am so blessed to have a Friend like you! I want to learn how to share more and more of my life with You. I believe You *are* capable of bringing beauty out of my lost dreams, Joy out of my sorrow, Peace out of my problems. However, I confess that often I get stuck in my brokenness and struggles. Help me bring all these things to You for transformation.

Beloved, you have made a request that pleases Me greatly. I delight in transforming My precious children. Give Me your broken dreams. Release them into My care and keeping. I will not only heal the brokenness, I will give you a new dream—one that is in harmony with My plans for you. As you seek to actualize this fresh dream, you will find yourself becoming more content and increasingly aware of My beautiful Presence.

Give Me also your sadness and your problems. Sorrow shared with Me is permeated with brilliant sparkles of Joy—like numerous Christmas lights glittering in the darkness. Accept adversity as My gift to you: Search for golden pockets of Peace hidden in the stony hardness of your problems.

I am your devoted Friend and also your King of kings, accomplishing My divine transformation in you. All things are possible with Me!

He has sent Me to bind up the brokenhearted...and provide for those who grieve in Zion—to bestow on them a crown of beauty instead of ashes, the oil of gladness instead of mourning, and a garment of praise instead of a spirit of despair. They will be called oaks of righteousness, a planting of the LORD for the display of his splendor.
Isaiah 61:1–3

Peace I leave with you; my peace I give you.
I do not give to you as the world gives.
Do not let your hearts be troubled and do not be afraid.
John 14:27

Jesus looked at them and said, "With man this is impossible, but with God all things are possible."
Matthew 19:26

I am always before you, beckoning you on—one step at a time. Neither height nor depth, nor anything else in all creation, can separate you from My loving Presence.

Dear Jesus,

I want to live my life focused on Your Presence in the present. I believe You are always before me, leading and encouraging me, but I need to live out of that reality moment by moment. My mind tends to leap over the present moment to the next task, ignoring the one that is before me and the One who is before me. During rare times when I am able to stay focused on You, my work is infused with Your Presence. It is no longer laborious but delightful: more like play than work.

Beloved, living in collaboration with Me can be a foretaste of heaven. It is wonderful, though not easy: It requires a level of spiritual and mental concentration that is extremely challenging. In the Psalms, David wrote about this collaborative way of living, declaring that he had set Me always before him.

As a shepherd, he had plenty of time to seek My Face and enjoy My Presence. He discovered the beauty of days lived with Me always before him—and beside him. I am training you to live this way too. This endeavor requires more persistent effort than anything else you have attempted. Yet, rather than detracting from your other activities, it fills them with vibrant Life.

Whatever you do, do it for Me—with Me, through Me, in Me. Even menial tasks glow with the Joy of My Presence when you do them for Me. Ultimately, nothing will be able to separate you from Me. So this you-and-I-together venture can continue throughout eternity.

For I am convinced that neither death nor life, neither angels nor demons, neither the present nor the future, nor any powers, neither height nor depth, nor anything else in all creation, will be able to separate us from the love of God that is in Christ Jesus our Lord.
Romans 8:38–39

I have set the LORD always before me.
Because he is at my right hand, I will not be shaken.
Psalm 16:8

And whatever you do, do it heartily, as to the Lord and not to men, knowing that from the Lord you will receive the reward of the inheritance; for you serve the Lord Christ.
Colossians 3:23-24 NKJV

> Invite Me into your thoughts by whispering
> My Name. Suddenly your day brightens
> and feels more user-friendly.

Dear Jesus,

When I speak Your Name in loving trust, I sense Your Presence and feel myself drawing closer to You. There is great Power in Your Name: I've found that simply whispering "Jesus" can turn a hard day into a good one. By calling upon Your Name frequently, I acknowledge my continual need of You.

Beloved, when you pray My Name, you are actually calling upon Me: My very Being. I joyfully respond to your invitation by coming nearer to you.

I am pleased by your desire to rely on Me in your small moments, as well as in the big events of your life. When you whisper My Name, I respond not only to your neediness but also to your love. As you look to Me, My Face shines upon you in radiant approval—brightening your day and helping you feel secure.

Salvation is found in no one else,
for there is no other name
under heaven given to men
by which we must be saved.
Acts 4:12

Come near to God and he
will come near to you.
James 4:8

And everyone who calls on the
name of the Lord will be saved.
Acts 2:21

The LORD make His face to shine upon
and enlighten you and be gracious
(kind, merciful, and giving favor) to you.
The LORD lift up His [approving] countenance
upon you and give you peace
[tranquility of heart and life continually].
Numbers 6:25–26 AMP

Nothing is wasted when you walk close to Me. Even your mistakes can be recycled into something good, through My transforming grace.

Dear Jesus,

I desperately want to believe that my mistakes can somehow be used for good in Your kingdom. The truth is, I hate making mistakes! This attitude can easily translate into hating myself for having messed up. When I let my mind run freely at such a time, I find myself fantasizing about *what might have been*—if only I had acted or chosen differently. I definitely need a strong dose of Your transforming grace!

Beloved, the best strategy for accepting yourself, even when you make mistakes, is living close to Me. This nearness helps you see things from My perspective. You tend to view yourself as someone who should be almost perfect, making very few errors. My perspective is quite different: I see you as My beloved child—weak in many ways, prone to wandering from

Me. However, your weakness and waywardness cannot diminish My constant Love for you. Moreover, My infinite wisdom enables Me to take your errors and weave them into an intricate work that is good.

You need to accept not only yourself but also the choices you have made. Fantasizing about having done things differently is a time-wasting trap. It is impossible to live close to Me while you're indulging in such unreality. The more you fantasize, the further from Me you wander. When you realize this has happened, turn around and run back to Me! Take time to talk with Me and relax in My Presence. Your perfectionist tendencies will dissolve as you soak in My transforming grace.

As a father has compassion on his children, so the LORD
has compassion on those who fear him; for he knows how
we are formed, he remembers that we are dust.
Psalm 103:13–14

May your unfailing love be my comfort,
according to your promise to your servant.
Psalm 119:76

In him we have redemption through his blood, the forgiveness
of sins, in accordance with the riches of God's grace that he
lavished on us with all wisdom and understanding.
Ephesians 1:7–8

> Marvel at the awesome wonder of being able to commune with the King of the universe any time, any place. Never take this amazing privilege for granted!

Dear Jesus,

I confess that often I do take this awesome prayer-privilege for granted. Even worse, at times I act as if I'm doing You a favor by spending time talking with You. Forgive me for my foolish arrogance!

Beloved, I am pleased that you recognize and repent of your foolishness. The best antidote to such thoughts is remembering who I Am: King of kings and Lord of lords, dwelling in dazzlingly unapproachable Light. My eyes are like blazing fire. My voice is like the sound of rushing waters. My face is like the sun shining in all its brilliance. I am also your Shepherd, tenderly leading you step by step through your life. I want you to realize how precious you are to Me—how much I delight in you. I long for you to reciprocate by delighting in Me.

I listen to your heart as well as to your words.
When you approach My throne of grace joyfully,
anticipating the wondrous pleasure of communing with
Me, both you and I are blessed!

God, the blessed and only Ruler, the King of kings
and Lord of lords, who alone is immortal and who lives in
unapproachable light, whom no one has seen or can see.
To him be honor and might forever. Amen.
1 Timothy 6:15–16

His head and hair were white like wool,
as white as snow, and his eyes were like blazing fire.
His feet were like bronze glowing in a furnace,
and his voice was like the sound of rushing waters.
In his right hand he held seven stars, and out
of his mouth came a sharp double-edged sword.
His face was like the sun shining in all its brilliance.
Revelation 1:14–16

Delight yourself in the LORD
and he will give you the desires of your heart.
Psalm 37:4

Let us then approach the throne of grace
with confidence, so that we may receive mercy
and find grace to help us in our time of need.
Hebrews 4:16

> Thank Me for the gift of My Peace: a gift of such immense proportions that you cannot fathom its depth or breadth.

Dear Jesus,

I have searched for Peace in many different places, but only Yours is real and enduring. Wonderful as Your Peace is, it often eludes me. When I let down my guard, anxiety creeps in without my permission. It tugs at the corners of my mind, drawing me away from awareness of You. Please teach me how to enjoy Your Peace more continually.

Beloved, you can thank Me for the gift of My Peace even when you're feeling anxious. My Peace is not so much a feeling as it is an unchangeable condition. It is permanent forgiveness: My eternal gift to you through My blood. I am not only the Giver of true Peace; I Myself am your Peace. It is every bit as available to you as I am. When you seek My Presence and find Me, you also encounter My Peace.

Thanking Me for the gift of My Peace, regardless of how you feel, is ultimately an act of trust. Your gratitude and trust will draw you closer to Me—the Lord of Peace. Rejoice as you explore with Me the immense proportions of My gift: Peace at all times and in every way!

For God was pleased to have all his fullness dwell in him,
and through him to reconcile to himself all things,
whether things on earth or things in heaven, by making
peace through his blood, shed on the cross.
Colossians 1:19–20

For he himself is our peace, who has made the two one
and has destroyed the barrier, the dividing wall of hostility.
Ephesians 2:14

Cast all your anxiety on him because he cares for you.
1 Peter 5:7

Now may the Lord of peace himself give you
peace at all times and in every way.
The Lord be with all of you.
2 Thessalonians 3:16

> I am the Creator of the universe,
> yet I choose to make My humble home
> in your heart. It is there where you know
> Me most intimately; it is there where
> I speak to you in holy whispers.

Dear Jesus,

This is more than I can fathom—that Someone so great and majestic would choose to live in someone so small and sinful. My mind almost recoils at the thought of Your perfect holiness living in me. Indeed, I am an exceedingly humble home for You. It helps to remember that though You live in me, You also inhabit the highest heavens. Someday I will behold You in the courts of heaven, where I will see You in all Your Glory.

I am thankful You are willing to live in my heart, because I deeply desire intimacy with You. However, I am weak: easily distracted by the noise of the world. Help me hear Your whispers in my heart.

Beloved, you do well to struggle with the thought of My holiness inhabiting your body. That shows Me you have some understanding of the absolute purity of My Being. Nonetheless, be assured that your sinfulness cannot taint My holiness. The influence goes the other direction: My righteousness purifies you! Delight in this blessed transaction, gratefully receiving My goodness.

You need stillness—outer and inner—to hear My gentle whispers in your heart. Find a quiet place, where the noise of the world is minimal. Then, focus your mind on this verse: "Cease striving and know that I am God." Be still, let go, and relax in My Presence, while I commune with you in holy whispers.

But in these last days he has spoken to us
by his Son, whom he appointed heir of all things,
and through whom he made the universe.
Hebrews 1:2

I pray that out of his glorious riches he may strengthen you
with power through his Spirit in your inner being,
so that Christ may dwell in your hearts through faith.
Ephesians 3:16–17

After the earthquake came a fire, but the LORD was not
in the fire. And after the fire came a gentle whisper.
1 Kings 19:12

Cease striving and know that I am God....
Psalm 46:10 NASB

Although self-sufficiency is acclaimed
in the world, reliance on Me produces
abundant living in My kingdom.

Dear Jesus,

Walking to the world's tempo is tempting at times.
The desire to *blend in* can be both subtle and powerful.
Self-sufficiency is certainly promoted in the world,
sometimes to the point of self-deification. Though I
don't really want to *be* self-sufficient, I sometimes find
myself trying to appear as if I am. I know better: I have
discovered that depending on You is the way to live
more abundantly. Whenever I face difficult situations,
I am grateful I can rely on You to help me. Teach me to
depend on You more and more.

Beloved, the first thing you must deal with is being
overly concerned about appearances. Remember
that I look at your heart, not your outward appearance.
What is most important to Me should also be most
important to you. Resist the desire to look good and
blend in with the world. Recognize that most people

who appear self-sufficient are actually struggling deeply; many are even dependent on harmful substances to help them keep up appearances.

Reliance on Me results in abundant living because it is the way I designed you to live: I created people to be dependent on Me. The essence of Adam and Eve's first sin was their desire to be *like God* and thus capable of living independently. Ever since then, depending on Me continually has gone against the grain of human nature. Notice I said "continually"; this is the way I want you to rely on Me. Depending on Me in difficult circumstances is a good start. However, the more frequently you look to Me for help, the more you will find Me faithful. I sustain you moment by moment, so there is never a time when you don't need Me. Awareness of your neediness is actually a rich blessing— connecting you to Me and My abundant supply!

The LORD does not look at the things man looks at. Man looks at
the outward appearance, but the LORD looks at the heart.
1 Samuel 16:7

"You will not surely die," the serpent said …
"you will be like God, knowing good and evil."
Genesis 3:4–5

I have set the LORD continually before me;
because He is at my right hand, I shall not be moved.
Psalm 16:8 AMP

I comprehend you in all your complexity;
no detail of your life is hidden from Me.
I view you through eyes of grace, so don't
be afraid of My intimate awareness.

Dear Jesus,

It is totally amazing that You understand me—all of me—with absolute accuracy. That could also be terrifying, if You saw me through eyes of law rather than grace. Unfortunately, I often view myself legalistically: evaluating how well I'm performing. I realize how silly that is, because my performance will always be insufficient to meet Your holy standard. That's why I desperately need Your grace! Please help me see myself, as well as others, through eyes of grace.

Beloved, come to Me and receive My unfailing Love. You are troubled by fear of failure, but My Love for you will never fail. Let Me describe what I see, as I view you through eyes of grace. You look regal, for I have clothed you in My royal righteousness. You also look radiant, especially when you are gazing at Me. You are lovely as you reflect My Glory back to Me. In fact, you delight Me so much that I rejoice over you with shouts of Joy! This is how you appear through My vision of grace.

Because I am infinite, I can see you simultaneously as you are now and as you will be in heaven. The present view helps Me work with you on things you need to change. The heavenly vision enables Me to love you with perfect, everlasting Love.

The best way to see through eyes of grace is to look through the lens of My unfailing Love. As you persevere in this practice, you will gradually find it easier to extend grace both to yourself and to others.

How priceless is your unfailing love!
Both high and low among men
find refuge in the shadow of your wings.
Psalm 36:7

I sought the LORD, and he answered me; he delivered me
from all my fears. Those who look to him are radiant;
their faces are never covered with shame.
Psalm 34:4–5

The LORD your God is in your midst,...
He will exult over you with joy,...
He will rejoice over you with shouts of joy.
Zephaniah 3:17 NASB

> Do not be afraid, for I am with you.
> Hear Me saying, "Peace, be still!"
> to your restless heart.

Dear Jesus,

Fearfulness seems to come so naturally to me, as if it's the default setting when I let my thoughts run freely. Peacefulness, on the other hand, requires continual effort and a degree of vigilance. I need to stay aware of Your Presence with me, to quiet my anxious heart. I confess I often lose sight of You, as the visible world lures my attention away from Your unseen Reality.

Beloved, I understand how vulnerable you are to things that impact your senses. It's good that you, too, are aware of this weakness. Also, you recognize that I am the answer to your vulnerability. This condition of yours is ever so human: The visible world tugs at the heartstrings of all My children. Because of this common human tendency, My Word exhorts you to be alert and prayerful—fixing your eyes on Me, bringing every thought captive to Me.

The sounds of the world (as well as its sights) tend to lead you away from Me. You need a quiet place in order to hear My voice. As you listen intently in My Presence, I guide your mind to think My thoughts. Bring Me your restless heart, and wait while I speak Peace into its depths—stilling the troubled waters of your soul.

Then He arose and rebuked the wind,
and said to the sea, "Peace, be still!"
And the wind ceased, and there was a great calm.
Mark 4:39 NKJV

And pray in the Spirit on all occasions
with all kinds of prayers and requests. With this in mind,
be alert and always keep on praying for all the saints.
Ephesians 6:18

Let us fix our eyes on Jesus, the author and
perfecter of our faith, who for the joy set before
him endured the cross, scorning its shame,
and sat down at the right hand of the throne of God.
Hebrews 12:2

We demolish arguments and every pretension that sets
itself up against the knowledge of God, and we take
captive every thought to make it obedient to Christ.
2 Corinthians 10:5

As you live in close contact with Me,
the Light of My Presence filters through
you to bless others. Your weakness and
woundedness are openings through
which the Light of the knowledge
of My Glory shines forth.

Dear Jesus,

You are absolutely perfect in all Your ways! It's awesome that You want to live in close contact with me, because You and I both know how flawed I am. I wish I could bring You a more cleaned-up version of myself, but I know better than to try pretending with You. So I come near You just as I am: weak and wounded.

Beloved, your honesty and vulnerability draw Me closer to you. Feel the Light of My Presence shining upon you and within you. Let these healing rays soak deep into your being. I want you to both receive My blessing and be a source of blessing to other people. The very things that trouble you most—your weaknesses and wounds—are of greatest use to Me in helping others.

I have shone into your heart the Light of the knowledge of the Glory revealed in My Face. That much Light and Glory simply cannot be contained within you! Your weaknesses and wounds provide openings through which some of this glorious Light spills out of you. By letting these humble, hurting parts of you be exposed, you bless others—as My Light shines through you into their lives. Thus, your weakness and woundedness, consecrated to Me, become treasures in My kingdom.

For God, who said, "Let light shine out of darkness,"
made his light shine in our hearts to give us the light of
the knowledge of the glory of God in the face of Christ.
2 Corinthians 4:6

Blessed are those who have learned to acclaim you,
who walk in the light of your presence, O LORD.
Psalm 89:15

But we have this treasure in jars of clay to show that this
all-surpassing power is from God and not from us.
We are hard pressed on every side, but not crushed;
perplexed, but not in despair; persecuted, but not
abandoned; struck down, but not destroyed.
2 Corinthians 4:7–9

Remember that I can fit everything into a pattern for good, including the things you wish were different. Start with where you are at this point in time and space, accepting that this is where I intend you to be.

Dear Jesus,

How I long to see this all-embracing pattern for good! I can't begin to imagine how You can fit everything into such a pattern. My current situation seems like a gigantic mistake to me: something I should have been able to prevent. I'm trying to accept my circumstances as Your will, but I feel as if I'm clawing my way up a sheer cliff. Help me make a new beginning, right where I am.

Beloved, even if I showed you the all-encompassing pattern, you wouldn't be able to understand it. Some things—many things—are simply beyond your comprehension. Do not indulge in obsessing about what you could have done differently, for that is an exercise in unreality: The past cannot be different from what has actually occurred.

There is only one place to make a new beginning, and that is NOW: the unique intersection of time and space you currently inhabit. I believe you can accept the present moment without too much difficulty. After all, you are conversing with Me, your Savior and Shepherd, this very moment. You can also handle the next moment as it comes—and the next. What you find most difficult to accept is the way the future looks to you: basing your predictions on current circumstances. But the future is one of those *secret things* beyond your domain; release it to Me, the rightful Owner. Refuse to worry about the future, and you will find your resources for today quite sufficient. Remember that I am part of those resources, and nothing is impossible with Me!

We are assured and know that [God being a partner in their labor] all things work together and are [fitting into a plan] for good to and for those who love God and are called according to [His] design and purpose.
Romans 8:28 AMP

The secret things belong to the LORD our God, but the things revealed belong to us and to our children forever, that we may follow all the words of this law.
Deuteronomy 29:29

For nothing is impossible with God.
Luke 1:37

> Rather than planning and evaluating,
> practice trusting and thanking Me
> continually. This is a paradigm shift that
> will revolutionize your life.

Dear Jesus,

You certainly know me well! When my mind is idle, it veers toward planning and evaluating. I seem to be addicted to planning. I think it's a way I try to feel more peaceful, but it actually has the opposite effect: increasing anxiety. Evaluating also seems to be second nature to me—as if it's my responsibility to pass judgment on everything and everyone. Please help me break free of these harmful tendencies.

Beloved, an effective way of dealing with addictions is to substitute good responses for the harmful behavior. When you find yourself flitting down your well-worn path of planning, stop and affirm your trust in Me. It can be as simple as saying, "I trust You, Jesus, to help me with this." Remember that I will be with you at that future time, helping you make decisions when needed. So, you can substitute affirmations of trust for compulsive planning. As you do so, your anxiety level will drop dramatically.

Your sense of responsibility to make judgments about everything is both hurtful and distorted. This attitude easily deteriorates into criticizing and complaining. Though you may not realize it, much of this negativity is ultimately directed at Me—the One who is sovereign over all things. Thankful words are the best replacements for your criticisms and complaints. There are always so many things you can thank Me for, especially My provision of eternal Life. As you practice trusting and thanking Me, the quality of your life will improve immensely.

Changing your thought patterns requires time and mental discipline. However, the results are well worth the effort: Your thankful, trusting attitude will bring good pleasure to Me and abundant blessing to you.

Humble yourselves, therefore, under God's mighty hand, that he may lift you up in due time. Cast all your anxiety on him because he cares for you.
1 Peter 5:6–7

The LORD gives strength to his people;
the LORD blesses his people with peace.
Psalm 29:11

"Do not judge, or you too will be judged."
Matthew 7:1

> Look for a star of guidance in your life,
> and be willing to follow wherever
> I lead. I am the Light from on high
> that dawns upon you, to guide your
> feet into the way of Peace.

Dear Jesus,

I so long to walk in the way of Peace, and I believe that You are the only Way. I ask that Your Light may shine upon me more and more. I continually need the Light of Your Presence, because I live in a cold, dark world. I desire Your radiant Presence not only for warmth but also for guidance. Please lead me along the path of Peace.

Beloved, My Presence radiates Light that helps you find the way of Peace. My Word enlightens your mind and heart, empowering you to stay on the right path. As you read Scripture, look for a star of guidance. Ask My Spirit to illumine those words to your seeking heart. They are words of Life!

Remember that I am your Shepherd. To walk in the way of Peace, you must follow Me wholeheartedly. If you drift even slightly from following My lead, you are at risk. For a while you will still be able to see Me, as you go your own way "just a bit." Eventually, however, you will lose sight of Me altogether. Veering even a few degrees off course will ultimately take you far from Me. With your feet no longer on the path of Peace, you will find yourself becoming increasingly anxious. The most important thing at this point is to realize you have lost your way. If you are humble enough, you can call out to Me for help. I am near to all who call on Me. I will hear your cry and save you, leading you back to the way of Peace.

A Light from on high will dawn upon us and visit [us],
To shine upon and give light to those who sit
in darkness and in the shadow of death, to direct
and guide our feet in a straight line into the way of peace.
Luke 1:78–79 AMP

Jesus answered, "I am the way and the truth and the life.
No one comes to the Father except through me."
John 14:6

Your word is a lamp to my feet and a light for my path.
Psalm 119:105

The LORD is near to all who call on him, to all who call on him
in truth. He fulfills the desires of those who fear him;
he hears their cry and saves them.
Psalm 145:18–19

> What I search for in My children is an awakened soul that thrills to the Joy of My Presence! I created mankind to glorify and enjoy Me forever. I provide the Joy; your part is to glorify Me by living close to Me.

Dear Jesus,

I long to have a fully awakened soul! I've discovered that nothing is more satisfying than the Joy of your Presence. However, I'm often subject to a slumbering soul: taking for granted my life with all its blessings, being overly focused on negative things, buying into the world's version of the good life. Help me break free from these worldly weights, so my soul can soar in the heights with You.

Beloved, the fact that you yearn for an awakened soul is itself a source of pleasure to Me. Many of My children view devotion to Me as a duty, and they look elsewhere for their pleasures. They fail to understand that the Joy of My Presence outshines even the most delightful earthly joy. Of course, it is not an either/or situation. You don't have to choose between enjoying Me or enjoying the many good gifts I provide. It is simply a matter of priorities: I want you to treasure Me above all else. Actually, the more fully you enjoy Me, the more capacity you have to appreciate the blessings I shower upon you. When you make Me your ultimate Pleasure, you glorify Me by desiring closeness with Me. As you delight in Me, I am free to bless you with many things that please you. If you keep Me first in your life, My good gifts will not become idols. Delight yourself in Me, and I will give you the desires and secret petitions of your heart.

For the eyes of the LORD range throughout the earth
to strengthen those whose hearts are fully committed to him.
2 Chronicles 16:9

You have made known to me the paths of life;
you will fill me with joy in your presence.
Acts 2:28

Every good and perfect gift is from above,
coming down from the Father of the heavenly lights,
who does not change like shifting shadows.
James 1:17

Delight yourself also in the LORD, and He will give you the desires
and secret petitions of your heart.
Psalm 37:4 AMP

> The intimacy I offer you is not an invitation to act as if you were My equal. Worship Me as King of kings while walking hand in hand with Me down the path of Life.

Dear Jesus,

I know I often treat You with less reverence than You deserve, especially when I'm upset with the way things are going in my life. When I'm hurting, I look for someone to blame—and sometimes it is You. Forgive me for rebelling against You and Your ways. Thank You for the amazing privilege of knowing You intimately.

Beloved, I took a huge risk when I created mankind in My own image. I made you with the potential to reverence and love Me freely, without coercion. In doing so, I gave you freedom to treat Me as an equal— or worse. I paid enormously for your freedom—with My own blood. This payment has made it possible for you to know Me—the King of kings and Lord of lords. When one of My children draws near to Me in reverent awe, I open My heart and offer intimate friendship. The Joy we share in one another cannot be measured.

From time to time you overstep your bounds, forgetting who I Am. You talk to Me carelessly, even slanderously. Our intimacy is hindered by your irreverent attitude, but My Love for you is constant. When you remember My majestic Presence and return to Me repentantly, I rush to meet you and enfold you in My embrace. I celebrate with you the Joy of being close again, as we walk together down the path of Life.

Until the appearing of our Lord Jesus Christ,
which God will bring about in his own time—God, the
blessed and only Ruler, the King of kings and Lord of lords.
1 Timothy 6:14–15

Jesus said to them, "Most assuredly,
I say to you, before Abraham was, I AM."
John 8:58 NKJV

So he got up and went to his father. But while he was still a long way
off, his father saw him and was filled with compassion for him; he
ran to his son, threw his arms around him and kissed him.
Luke 15:20

> Instead of single-mindedly pursuing a goal, talk with Me about it. Let the Light of My Presence shine on this pursuit, so you can see it from My perspective.

Dear Jesus,

Pursuing goals comes almost as naturally to me as breathing. When a goal grabs my attention, my instinct is to go for it, without really thinking it through. I may invest a lot of time and energy in something, only to realize later that it was the wrong pursuit. When I take the time to first discuss matters with You, my life is much more satisfying.

Beloved, there are many benefits to talking with Me—before, during, and after pursuing a goal. The Light of My Presence illuminates your pursuit, so you can see it more clearly. As you talk it over with Me, you gain a new perspective on the endeavor. The most important change in your perspective is a growing desire to please Me. This desire produces benefits far beyond the task at hand: It deepens your relationship with Me.

If you discern that your goal accords with My will, then you can pursue it confidently. As you work collaboratively with Me, continue to communicate about what you are doing. When the goal has been reached, thank Me for My help and guidance. Rejoice in what we have accomplished together!

Blessed are those who have learned to acclaim you,
who walk in the light of your presence, O LORD.
They rejoice in your name all day long;
they exult in your righteousness.
Psalm 89:15–16

There are many plans
in a man's heart, nevertheless
the LORD's counsel—that will stand.
Proverbs 19:21 NKJV

Commit your way to the LORD,
Trust also in Him, and He will do it.
Psalm 37:5 NASB

I can do all things through Him who strengthens me.
Philippians 4:13 NASB

> I am not a careless God. When I allow difficulties to come into your life, I equip you fully to handle them.

Dear Jesus,

I know You are perfect in all Your ways, so it is impossible for You to be careless. However, I also know You are absolutely sovereign: Nothing happens that You have not allowed. When difficulties in my life overwhelm me—events You could have prevented—sometimes it feels as if You are being careless with me. I believe You do equip me to handle whatever comes my way, but I need Your help in using the *equipment*.

Beloved, realizing you need My help is half the battle. You also need My Word and My Spirit. The Bible imparts to you essential wisdom: My promises to be near you and take care of you, exhortations that help you avoid sinful snares, offers of forgiveness when you "miss the mark," promises of My Spirit's living in you and empowering you.

It is important not to be surprised or alarmed by the many trials that enter your life. Until you reach your ultimate home in heaven, you will be at war. When you have a wartime mentality, it's easier to handle difficulties as they arise: You don't waste time and energy bemoaning your circumstances; you avoid the trap of feeling singled out for hardship.

I do indeed equip you fully to handle your difficulties. But you have to make the effort to use what I provide: My Presence, My Word, My Spirit. Come to Me when you are heavy laden and you will find rest for your soul.

So do not fear, for I am with you; do not be dismayed,
for I am your God. I will strengthen you and help you;
I will uphold you with my righteous right hand.
Isaiah 41:10

Be self-controlled and alert. Your enemy the devil prowls
around like a roaring lion looking for someone to devour.
Resist him, standing firm in the faith, because you know
that your brothers throughout the world are undergoing
the same kind of sufferings.
1 Peter 5:8–9

Come to Me, all you who labor and are heavy laden...
and you will find rest for your souls.
Matthew 11:28–29 NKJV

Spend time with Me for the pure pleasure of being in My company. I can brighten up the dullest of gray days; I can add sparkle to the routines of daily life.

Dear Jesus,

Spending time in Your company, keenly aware of Your Presence, is utterly delightful. It's a foretaste of the eternal pleasures You have prepared for me. However, I confess that the "dailyness" of life tends to pull me down: My focus on routine duties obscures my awareness of You. I want to enjoy Your continual Presence in all that I do.

Beloved, wait in My Presence while I reveal Myself to you. Put aside thoughts of tasks awaiting you, as you focus pleasurably on Me. Allow awareness of My Presence to become imprinted on your consciousness. Then move gently from this contemplative time into your routine duties. Refuse to view this part of your life as boring. Instead, continue communing with Me, asking Me to be vibrantly involved in your work.

Having already connected with Me at a deep level, you can find Me more easily in the midst of your activities. Naturally, you will lose sight of Me at times; I know you're only human. But you can reconnect readily, by moving toward Me in your thoughts, words, and feelings. The more you include Me in your awareness, the brighter your day will be: Your routines will sparkle with the liveliness of My company.

I wait for the LORD, my soul waits, and in his word I put my hope.
My soul waits for the Lord more than watchmen wait for the
morning, more than watchmen wait for the morning.
Psalm 130:5–6

As a father has compassion on his children, so the
LORD has compassion on those who fear him; for he
knows how we are formed, he remembers that we are dust.
Psalm 103:13–14

"For in him we live and move and have our being."
As some of your own poets have said, "We are his offspring."
Acts 17:28

As you give yourself more and more
to a life of constant communion with
Me, you will find that you simply
have no time for worry.

Dear Jesus,

I hate to say it, but I always find time for worrying!
I have battled this worry-beast for years, with little
success. Trying not to worry is like trying not to think
about something: The more I try, the more anxious I
become. I definitely need Your help in this battle.

Beloved, you do need My help, because trying
to fight this battle on your own has been so
counterproductive: Now you're worrying about
worrying! Your best strategy is to stop focusing on this
problem and put your energy into communicating more
with Me. This approach will help you achieve freedom
from all sorts of negative tendencies, including worry.
The idea is to replace hurtful, self-defeating behavior
with something wondrously positive—communicating
with your Creator and Savior.

Because I am your Creator, I know how you function best: I designed you for rich communion with Me. As your Savior, I also know how you function worst. Remember that I died for every one of your sins. Don't just talk to Me; listen to Me as well. I speak to you through My Word, My Spirit, My creation. As you give yourself more and more to communicating with Me, you will find your worry-time vanishing.

Who of you by worrying can add a single hour to
his life? Since you cannot do this very little thing,
why do you worry about the rest?
Luke 12:25–26

An anxious heart weighs a man down, but
a kind word cheers him up.
Proverbs 12:25

Show me your ways, O LORD,
teach me your paths;
guide me in your truth and teach me,
for you are God my Savior,
and my hope is in you all day long.
Psalm 25:4–5

Be unceasing in prayer [praying perseveringly].
1 Thessalonians 5:17 AMP

> Entrust your loved ones to Me.
> Release them into My protective care.
> They are much safer with Me than
> in your clinging hands.

Dear Jesus,

I think I sometimes confuse loving others with rescuing them. When a loved one has a problem, I often feel responsible to come up with a solution. I plunge headlong into problem-solving mode, as if I'm obligated to provide sound advice. Please help me stop feeling responsible to fix people, since that is Your role—not mine.

Beloved, it is indeed My prerogative to bring about change in people's lives, as I choose to do so. You can be part of the process, but remember that I am the Author and Director of the drama: You need to follow My script, rather than creating your own. Do not usurp My role in people's lives, no matter how much you long to help them.

When you feel compelled to rescue a loved one, take a good look at the quality of your love. Learn from Me, because I have all authority in heaven and on earth: I could rescue or control anyone at will. Yet I intentionally created people with the capacity to choose good or evil. I wanted them to be free to love Me—or not. Love that has no choice is not real!

Subordinate your deficient, controlling love to My perfect, empowering Love. Prayerfully release your loved ones to Me. Restrain your urges to solve their problems. Instead, use your time and energy to listen to them and pray for them. Trust in My Love and My unsearchable wisdom. I can work changes in your loved ones' lives: beyond anything you might ask or imagine. As you release these precious ones to Me, linger a while in My unfailing Love—for them and also for you.

Then Jesus came to them and said, "All authority in heaven and on earth has been given to me."
Matthew 28:18

Now to him who is able to do immeasurably more than all we ask or imagine, according to his power that is at work within us, to him be glory in the church and in Christ Jesus throughout all generations for ever and ever! Amen.
Ephesians 3:20–21

Let the morning bring me word of your unfailing love, for I have put my trust in you. Show me the way I should go, for to you I lift up my soul.
Psalm 143:8

> Waiting, trusting, and hoping are intricately connected: like golden strands interwoven to form a strong chain. Trusting is the central strand, because it is the response from My children that I desire the most.

Dear Jesus,

Often I feel as if waiting is what I do most of the time. I admit that it is difficult for me to wait: I prefer to make things happen myself, without delay. Hoping feels very similar to waiting; it is all about future things that are beyond my control. However, I have found that when I'm actively trusting You, waiting and hoping flow naturally out of my closeness with You.

Beloved, trusting Me is crucial, and it gives meaning to your waiting and hoping. Without trust, your connection with Me quickly deteriorates. That's why the Bible contains so many commands to trust Me. As you affirm your faith in Me, I empower you to wait with positive expectations. Waiting on Me is actually a great privilege, full of promise and blessing. Waiting on royalty has always been considered a high position, because it involves nearness to the royal persons. Ladies-in-waiting may perform humble services, such as helping people dress; yet these helpers are highly esteemed, even though they serve sinful, mortal royals. How much more should you treasure the privilege of serving Me—the King of eternity, immortal, invisible, the only God!

Hoping can be a joyful occupation, because it connects you to your promised inheritance in heaven. Such hope provides a rock-solid foundation in the present, helping you face the daily struggles of living in a broken world. Hope also connects you with Me, for I am the God of hope. My death on the cross opened the way for you to join My royal family and live with Me forever.

Trust in him at all times, O people; pour out your hearts
to him, for God is our refuge.
Psalm 62:8

Now to the King eternal, immortal, invisible,
the only God, be honor and glory for ever and ever. Amen.
1 Timothy 1:17

May the God of hope fill you with all joy and peace as you trust in him
so that you may overflow with hope by the power of the Holy Spirit.
Romans 15:13

> I know the depth and breadth of your need
> for Me. I can read the emptiness of your
> thoughts when they wander away from Me.

Dear Jesus,

The longer I live, the more I recognize how
desperately I need You. I want You to be central in
my life. However, I am easily distracted: My thoughts
wander away from You as readily as water flows
downhill. I need Your help *all the time*.

Beloved, recognizing the extent of your neediness
is one of your strengths. Humans can be divided
into two categories: needy people who recognize their
insufficiencies and needy people unaware of their
inadequacies.

Recognition, however, is only half the battle. The
other half is turning to Me—rather than idolatrous
substitutes—to fill your emptiness. Though substitutes
may seem appealing, they provide no lasting satisfaction.

Wandering thoughts are ever so human. Your
thoughts and feelings are constantly influenced by

the heaviness of this fallen world. As long as you live
on earth you will have to contend with this spiritual-
emotional "gravity" pulling you away from Me.
Thankfully, returning your thoughts to Me is not
as laborious as carrying water back uphill would be.
A short prayer in My Name is usually sufficient to
reconnect with Me, for I am never far from you. Indeed,
I have promised to be with you always—perpetually,
uniformly, and on every occasion—to the very close and
consummation of the age.

Put to death, therefore, whatever belongs to your
earthly nature: sexual immorality, impurity, lust,
evil desires and greed, which is idolatry.
Colossians 3:5

God did this so that men would seek him and perhaps reach out
for him and find him, though he is not far from each one of us.
Acts 17:27

Teaching them to observe everything that I have
commanded you, and behold, I am with you all the days
(perpetually, uniformly and on every occasion), to the [very]
close and consummation of the age. Amen (so let it be).
Matthew 28:20 AMP

As the Holy Spirit controls your mind and actions more fully, you become free in Me. You are increasingly released to become the one I created you to be.

Dear Jesus,

This sounds like a contradiction: becoming free through being controlled. Yet I know that when Your Spirit is controlling my thinking and behavior, I feel more alive—more real! You have taught me to pray, "Holy Spirit, think through me, live through me, love through me." I've found I am most content when I intentionally yield to You: inviting You to live through me. Nonetheless, my desire to be in control and do things my way often sabotages me.

Beloved, in My kingdom freedom comes from yielding to My will, which is perfect. Because I am infinite and you are not, My will may appear to be anything but perfect. I want you to trust Me at all times, even when you cannot understand what I'm doing. The Holy Spirit will help you in this, as you invite Him to control your thinking. He lives in the depths of your spirit, and He knows you better than you know yourself. His work in you can liberate you to become more completely the one I designed you to be. The Spirit and I work together in perfect harmony.

I am pleased when you ask My Spirit to think, live, and love through you. This is the collaborative way of living I had in mind when I created mankind. The more you collaborate with the Spirit, the freer you become: free to live exuberantly, to love extravagantly, to know Me in ever-increasing intimacy!

The mind of sinful man is death, but the mind
controlled by the Spirit is life and peace.
Romans 8:6

Do not conform any longer to the pattern of this world,
but be transformed by the renewing of your mind.
Then you will be able to test and approve what God's will is—
his good, pleasing and perfect will.
Romans 12:2

In the same way, the Spirit helps us in our weakness.
We do not know what we ought to pray for, but the Spirit
himself intercedes for us with groans that words cannot
express. And he who searches our hearts knows the mind
of the Spirit, because the Spirit intercedes for the saints
in accordance with God's will.
Romans 8:26–27

> I am ever so near you, hovering over your shoulder, reading every thought. People think that thoughts are fleeting and worthless, but yours are precious to Me.

Dear Jesus,

This is glorious—yet disconcerting! My thinking is not only the part of me that feels most hidden and secret; it is also the most difficult part of my behavior to master. In relationships with other people I can interact with them while keeping my secret thoughts to myself. Your ability to read my every thought is alarming, but it is also wonderful. It's a relief that there is Someone from whom I cannot hide: Secretiveness breeds loneliness. Moreover, the fact that You care about every aspect of me—even all my thoughts—demonstrates how important I am to You.

Beloved, I know how difficult it is for you to control your thoughts. Your mind is a battleground, and evil spirits work tirelessly to influence your thinking: even deceiving you with intrusive thoughts at times. Your own sinfulness also finds ample expression in your thoughts. You need to stay alert and fight against evil! I fought and died for you, so remember who you are and Whose you are. Thus, you put on the helmet of salvation. This helmet not only protects your mind, it also reminds you of the victory I secured for you on the cross.

Your thoughts are precious to Me because you are My treasure. As soon as your thinking turns My way, I notice and rejoice. The more thoughts you bring to Me, the more you can share in My Joy. I disarm evil thoughts and render them powerless. Then I help you think about things that are true, noble, right, pure, lovely, admirable—excellent and praiseworthy things. Ponder these things, while resting in the Peace of My Presence.

O LORD, you have searched me and you know me. You know when I sit and when I rise; you perceive my thoughts from afar.
Psalm 139:1–2

Take the helmet of salvation and the sword of the Spirit, which is the word of God.
Ephesians 6:17

Finally, brother, whatever is true, whatever is noble, whatever is right, whatever is pure, whatever is lovely, whatever is admirable— if anything is excellent or praiseworthy—think about such things.
Philippians 4:8

I have prepared this day with the most tender concern and attention to detail. Instead of approaching the day as a blank page you need to fill up, try living it in a responsive mode: being on the lookout for all that I am doing.

Dear Jesus,

This is the way I want to live—discovering what You are doing, and responding to the opportunities You place before me. I know this is the most joyful and productive way to live. Nonetheless, the part of me that likes being in control resists this manner of living. Please teach me the art of living responsively.

Beloved, because I am your Creator, I am the Initiator of your very life. Your first cry as an infant was a response to the life I provided. Many people think they can live independently of Me, but that is an illusion. I sustain everything by My powerful word! When I cease sustaining someone's life, that person dies. So, living responsively is a matter of aligning yourself with ultimate reality: My sovereignty over the universe. The fact that I am sovereign over every aspect of your life can increase your sense of security, to the extent that you trust in My perfect Love. Thus, the art of living responsively rests upon a foundation of trust—in My absolute goodness, My infinite wisdom, My loving Presence.

To build on this trust-foundation, you need to be perceptive: seeing things from My perspective as well as yours. Search for what I am doing in the big picture as well as in the details of your day. Living this way requires concentration, because the world is rigged to distract you from Me. However, the times when you do succeed in living responsively will be the best in your life: You will feel fully alive and richly connected with Me at such times. This is a foretaste of what awaits you in heaven, where you will respond to Me perfectly—throughout eternity!

The Son is the radiance of God's glory and the exact representation of his being, sustaining all things by his powerful word.
Hebrews 1:3

Are not two sparrows sold for a penny? Yet not one of them will fall to the ground apart from the will of your Father. And even the very hairs of your head are all numbered. So don't be afraid; you are worth more than many sparrows.
Matthew 10:29–31

But I trust in your unfailing love; my heart rejoices in your salvation.
Psalm 13:5

> Trouble and distress are woven into the very fabric of this perishing world. Only My Life in you can empower you to face this endless flow of problems with good cheer.

Dear Jesus,

I confess that *good cheer* does not describe my usual attitude when I'm faced with multiple problems. Difficulties tend to become my focus, obscuring my view of You. I know in my head that the world is in a state of brokenness, but my heart still yearns for a problem-free life. Help me to be realistic about the condition of this world without succumbing to despair.

Beloved, you need to remember that this fallen world is temporary: It is perishing! The world is not your true home; thus, it's normal for you to feel uncomfortable in it. The yearnings of your heart point to your real, eternal home, so do not squelch those longings. Instead, let them serve as reminders that your ultimate destination is heaven. Nonetheless, I do want you to live well in this world for as long as I keep you here.

I have not left you to handle by yourself the trouble and distress of this life. I have poured My very Being into you, in the Person of the Holy Spirit. Make plenty of space in your heart for this glorious One. Let Him empower you to live above your circumstances. I am telling you these things so that you can experience My Peace in the midst of a problem-filled life. You will continue to have trials and frustration in this world, but be of good cheer. I have overcome the world.

In my Father's house are many rooms;
if it were not so, I would have told you.
I am going there to prepare a place for you.
John 14:2

And I will ask the Father, and he will give you another
Counselor to be with you forever—the Spirit of truth...
for he lives with you and will be in you.
John 14:16–17

These things I have spoken to you, that in Me you
may have peace. In the world you will have tribulation;
but be of good cheer, I have overcome the world.
John 16:33 NKJV

Anxiety wraps you up in yourself, trapping you in your own thoughts. When you look to Me and whisper My Name, you break free and receive My help.

Dear Jesus,

You understand me so well. When I'm feeling anxious, I lose the ability to think clearly. My thoughts spin out of control with ever-increasing velocity. This sets me on a downward spiral of increasing anxiety and runaway thoughts. At such times, it's hard to remember You are with me—ready to help.

Beloved, I know how difficult it is for you to break free when you are trapped in anxious thoughts. That's why I encourage you to change the subject by whispering My Name: "Jesus." The very simplicity of this act makes it possible to do—even when you're not thinking clearly. There is immense Power in My Name to help you break free from the anxiety closing in on you. When you speak My Name, however quietly, you acknowledge My continual Presence. This truth is promised to all My followers, and it sets you free. Freedom and My Presence make an excellent combination: enabling you to turn your thoughts into conversation with Me.

Begin by thanking Me for always hearing your prayers. Then, talk with Me about whatever is worrying you, trusting that I understand you and your situation perfectly. As you converse with Me, the weight of your burden shifts to My strong shoulders, enabling you to relax. Now you are ready to receive My help, which I continually offer you.

To the Jews who had believed him, Jesus said,
"If you hold to my teaching, you are really my disciples.
Then you will know the truth, and the truth will set you free."
John 8:31–32

Search me, O God, and know my heart;
test me and know my anxious thoughts.
Psalm 139:23

Let the beloved of the LORD rest secure in him, for he
shields him all day long, and the one the LORD loves
rests between his shoulders.
Deuteronomy 33:12

> As you come to Me and take My yoke upon
> you, I fill you with My very Life. This
> is how I choose to live in the world and
> accomplish My purposes; it is also how
> I bless you with inexpressible, glorious Joy.

Dear Jesus,

I delight in coming to You, but I'm not quite as eager to be yoked. That sounds restrictive, and I definitely like to feel free. However, I'm gradually learning that You do know what is best for me, even when it involves restrictions or suffering. I want to be filled with Your Life and Joy, so please show me how to take Your yoke upon me.

Beloved, the simplest way is to say yes to Me and My ways. I want you to be teachable. Receive My yoke as a teaching tool that helps you learn more and more about Me. Being yoked keeps you close to Me, on the path I have chosen for you. While this may feel restrictive at times, it protects you from many dangers.

As you live close to Me, My Life within you is nourished and strengthened. This enables Me to live more fully in you, accomplishing My purposes through you. I assure you, though, that I do not use you in a mechanistic way. There is a vibrant kinship between us as I live in and through you. This intimate connection produces immense Joy—far beyond anything the world can offer. The Joy I give is so wondrously glorious that it cannot be expressed in words.

My yoke is not harsh, hard, sharp, or pressing. On the contrary, it is comfortable, gracious, and pleasant. As you submit to these bonds of Love, I fill you with Life and Joy in overflowing abundance.

Take My yoke upon you and learn of Me, for I am gentle (meek) and humble (lowly) in heart, and you will find rest (relief and ease and refreshment and recreation and blessed quiet) for your souls. For My yoke is wholesome (useful, good—not harsh, hard, sharp or pressing, but comfortable, gracious and pleasant), and My burden is light and easy to be borne.
Matthew 11:29–30 AMP

Though you have not seen him, you love him; and even though you do not see him now, you believe in him and are filled with an inexpressible and glorious joy, for you are receiving the goal of your faith, the salvation of your souls.
1 Peter 1:8–9

I have told you this so that my joy may be in you and that your joy may be complete.
John 15:11

My Peace is such an all-encompassing gift
that it is independent of circumstances.
Though you lose everything else, if you gain
My Peace you are rich indeed.

Dear Jesus,

There are so many aspects of my life over which I have
no control. I often feel at the mercy of my circumstances.
Your all-encompassing Peace is exactly what I need!
Although Your Peace is a gift, I sometimes feel unable
to receive it. Perhaps that is because I cling to other
things—my loved ones, my possessions, my reputation.
Help me to treasure Your Peace above all of these.

Beloved, My Peace is a supernatural gift—bequeathed
to My followers shortly before My death. A man
who knows he will soon die wants to leave something
precious with those he loves. Therefore, I "willed" My
Peace to My disciples and all who follow Me. I knew
this was a difficult gift to receive, especially in the midst
of adversity. So, after My resurrection, the first words
I spoke to My disciples were "Peace be with you!" They

needed this reassurance, to reinforce what I taught them before I died. You also need to be reminded of the divine nature of this gift, for it is not the world's peace I give you: It is Peace that transcends all understanding!

Clinging to other things makes it hard for you to receive My precious gift. That is like wrapping your fingers tightly around a small copper coin, while I am offering you unlimited supplies of pure gold. To receive My proffered gift, you must first open your hands and your heart to Me. By doing so, you release your concerns into My care and keeping. As you receive My glorious Peace, you gain deeper intimacy with Me—the richest blessing of all!

Do not be anxious about anything, but in everything, by prayer
and petition, with thanksgiving, present your requests to God.
And the peace of God, which transcends all understanding,
will guard your hearts and your minds in Christ Jesus.
Philippians 4:6–7

Peace I leave with you; my peace I give you.
I do not give to you as the world gives.
Do not let your hearts be troubled and do not be afraid.
John 14:27

On the evening of that first day of the week, when the disciples
were together, with the doors locked for fear of the Jews,
Jesus came and stood among them and said, "Peace be with you!"
John 20:19

Let Me be your positive focus. When you look to Me, knowing Me as *God with you*, you experience Joy.

*D*ear *J*esus,

I am so thankful You are *God with us*—constantly, eternally. That knowledge alone is sufficient to fill my days with Joy. Sadly, though, my mind easily slips out of focus, and I forget about your abiding Presence. When my thinking is unfocused, almost anything can grab my attention. Then You slip even further from my awareness. Worries and worldliness attack my mind while it is idling, out of gear. I want You to be my positive focus, but I definitely need help.

*B*eloved, I created you in My image: with the capacity to communicate with Me. As My image-bearer, you have the ability to choose the focus of your mind. I understand that many thoughts come and go unbidden, but you can control your thinking more than you may realize. Under the inspiration of the Holy Spirit, Paul wrote, "Whatever is true, whatever is noble, whatever is right…think about such things." I would not instruct you to think about certain things unless it was possible to do so.

Because the world contains both good and evil, you can choose to think about excellent, praiseworthy things or about terrible, upsetting things. Sometimes, of course, you have to deal with the brokenness around you. However, each day contains moments when you are free to choose the focal point of your mind. These are the times when I want you to take charge of your thoughts. When your mind is idle, it often moves toward a negative focus—such as regretting things in your past or worrying about the future. Meanwhile, I am with you in the present: waiting for you to recall My Presence. Train your mind to turn toward Me frequently. Remembrance of who I Am can brighten even your darkest times, blessing you with Joy.

All this took place to fulfill what the Lord had said through the prophet: "The virgin will be with child and will give birth to a son and they will call him Immanuel"—which means "God with us."
Matthew 1:22–23

Finally, brothers, whatever is true, whatever is noble, whatever is right...think about such things.
Philippians 4:8

"I tell you the truth," Jesus answered, "before Abraham was born, I AM!"
John 8:58

Fear of man will prove to be a snare,
but whoever trusts in Me is kept safe.

Dear Jesus,

I'm just beginning to realize how much my life is hampered by fear of man. This condition has been so prevalent that I failed to recognize it most of my life; it was simply part of the fabric of my daily existence. Now that I recognize this fear, I want very much to be free of it. But it is deeply engrained in my mind and heart. When I am with people, I'm much too concerned about displeasing them or looking foolish in their eyes. I confess I am a people pleaser, but I deeply desire to change.

Beloved, I will give you a two-pronged approach for dealing with this crippling fear. First, replace your fear of displeasing people with dread of displeasing Me—the Lord of the universe. Make pleasing Me your highest priority. Include Me in your thinking whenever you are making plans or decisions. Let your desire to please Me shine brightly, illuminating your thoughts and choices.

The second way to free yourself from fear of man is by developing deeper trust in Me. Instead of trying to please people so they will give you what you want, trust in Me—the Supplier of all your needs. My glorious riches never run short, nor does My Love for you. People can easily deceive you, promising you things with no intention of following through. Even if they mean well at the time, they may change their minds later on. Because I remain the same forever, I am absolutely dependable. Trusting in people is risky. Trusting in Me is wise: It keeps you safe.

Fear of man will prove to be a snare,
but whoever trusts in the LORD is kept safe.
Proverbs 29:25

So we make it our goal to please him, whether
we are at home in the body or away from it.
2 Corinthians 5:9

And my God will meet all your needs according
to his glorious riches in Christ Jesus.
Philippians 4:19

But you remain the same, and
your years will never end.
Psalm 102:27

I love you regardless of how well you are performing. Bring your performance anxiety to Me, and receive in its place My unfailing Love.

Dear Jesus,

I know that performance anxiety is foolish and counterproductive. My mind has unmasked this robber of Peace many times, but the rascal continues to claw at my heart when I let down my guard. I find myself struggling with feelings of failure, sometimes without even knowing why. Help me break free from this bondage through the empowerment of Your Love.

Beloved, come to Me with your feelings of failure. Bring them into the Light of My Presence, where we can examine them together. In My brilliant Light, the feelings shrivel and shrink, because they are based on lies. These things thrive in the darkness, where you are hardly aware of them at all. Performance anxiety has been such a regular part of your life that you barely notice it. Yet I defeated that villain in the same way I triumphed over Satan—through My finished work on the cross!

When feelings of failure weigh you down, look up to Me! Let the Light of My unfailing Love shine upon you: dispelling the darkness, lifting you closer and closer to Me. The nearer you are to Me, the better you can see My smile of approval. As you bask in this unconditional Love, you gain strength to break free from your nemesis—performance anxiety. Even if you slip into old habits again, you can turn back to Me anytime. My unfailing Love is always available to restore you, because you belong to Me forever.

Turn, O LORD, and deliver me;
save me because of your unfailing love.
Psalm 6:4

How priceless is your unfailing love!
Both high and low among men
find refuge in the shadow of your wings.
They feast on the abundance of your house;
you give them drink from your river of delights.
For with you is the fountain of life;
in your light we see light.
Psalm 36:7–9

But thanks be to God! He gives us the victory
through our Lord Jesus Christ.
1 Corinthians 15:57

When you are weary and everything seems to be going wrong, you can still utter these four words: "I trust You, Jesus." By doing so, you release matters into My control, and you fall back into the security of My everlasting arms.

Dear Jesus,

It's so hard for me to release things into Your control, rather than trying to fix them myself. I recognize that ultimately this is a matter of trust. I know enough about You and enough about me to realize how ridiculous it would be to trust myself more than You. In the depths of my soul I do trust You far more than anyone or anything else. However, I tend to live on a surface level much of the time—living by sight more than by faith. Help me overcome my unbelief!

Beloved, that cry of your heart is a prayer I am eager to answer. I can see into the depths of your soul, where you do indeed trust Me. I am pleased that you recognize the discrepancy between the trust in your soul and the controllingness of your surface-level behavior. When you are living superficially, you tend to be unaware of your thoughts. As a result, you follow well-worn paths of habitual responses. In this condition of mental slumber, you are unable to hear My voice. As soon as you become aware of your condition, you need to speak to Me. You can say, "I trust You, Jesus," regardless of how you are feeling. Intentionally release your worries into My care and keeping—My control. You can even symbolize this release physically, by opening both hands fully to Me. Then, rest in the knowledge that I am taking care of you and all that concerns you. As you trustingly relax in My Presence, your mind reconnects with your soul. Find refreshment in the refuge of My everlasting arms.

The eternal God is your refuge,
and underneath are the everlasting arms.
Deuteronomy 33:27

Immediately the boy's father exclaimed,
"I do believe; help me overcome my unbelief!"
Mark 9:24

Commit your way to the LORD; trust in him and he will do this:
He will make your righteousness shine like the dawn,
the justice of your cause like the noonday sun.
Psalm 37:5–6

I hate it when My children grumble, casually despising My sovereignty. Thankfulness is a safeguard against this deadly sin. Furthermore, a grateful attitude becomes a grid through which you perceive life.

Dear Jesus,

I confess I am a grumbler. When things are not as I'd like them to be, my first impulse is to complain. Even if I manage to keep my mouth shut, I tend to grumble in my thoughts. Usually when I complain, it doesn't occur to me that I am opposing You and Your ways. It shocks me to realize that grumbling amounts to *casually despising Your sovereignty*. Forgive me, Lord!

Beloved, complaining is quite common among My children, but it is nonetheless a deadly sin. When the Israelites grumbled against their leader, Moses, I dealt with them severely. Though they may not have been aware of it, they were actually rebelling against Me, and I responded accordingly: All those complainers who were twenty or older died in the desert, never reaching the Promised Land.

The best safeguard against falling prey to grumbling is thankfulness. When gratitude fills your heart and mind, you will not be tempted to complain. My Word is seasoned with multiple commands to be thankful—for good reason! I ransomed you from eternal punishment through My torturous death on the cross. That alone is sufficient reason for thankfulness. However, I continue to shower additional blessings upon you. Work at developing a grateful mind-set, and you will be able to perceive My gifts more clearly. Gratitude also enables you to draw closer to Me. As you learn to give thanks in all circumstances, My loving Presence will increasingly brighten your vision of life.

Moses also said…"Who are we? You are not grumbling
against us, but against the LORD."
Exodus 16:8

In this desert your bodies will fall—every one of you
twenty years old or more…. who has grumbled against me.
Numbers 14:29

Give thanks in all circumstances,
for this is God's will for you in Christ Jesus.
1 Thessalonians 5:18

> Bearing your circumstances bravely—even
> thanking Me for them—is one of the
> highest forms of praise. This sacrifice of
> thanksgiving rings golden-toned bells of Joy
> throughout heavenly realms. On earth, also,
> your patient suffering sends out ripples of
> good tidings in ever-widening circles.

Dear Jesus,

You have been training me in the discipline of thankfulness for a long time. Yet I still find it quite challenging to thank You for suffering—my own or others'. Sometimes, though, I am able to thank You for painful circumstances. This seems unnatural at first, but it is actually quite freeing. When I am able to do this, I find that I relax and feel closer to You. Please help me endure my circumstances bravely—with gratitude.

Beloved, thanking Me for adversity requires a deep level of trust: in My goodness, My mercy, My Love. People who are leaning on their own understanding cannot achieve this depth of trust. So, handling difficulties courageously involves relinquishing your demand to understand.

You have experienced personal benefits from thanking Me for hard situations, but there is more— much more! Your grateful acceptance of adversity has major repercussions far beyond yourself: in heaven as well as on earth. Joy-bells resound in heavenly domains when suffering believers trust Me enough to give thanks. Also, your sacrifice of thanksgiving has divine Power to weaken spiritual strongholds of evil. Moreover, your patient endurance of suffering can strengthen and encourage My people on earth.

Sacrifice thank offerings to Me. Tell of My works with songs of Joy! (Psalm 107:22)

Always giving thanks to God the Father for
everything, in the name of our Lord Jesus Christ.
Ephesians 5:20

Trust in the LORD with all your heart
and lean not on your own understanding.
Proverbs 3:5

For though we live in the world, we do not wage war as the world
does. The weapons we fight with are not the weapons of the world.
On the contrary, they have divine power to demolish strongholds.
2 Corinthians 10:3–4

Holiness is letting Me live through you.
Since I dwell in you, you are fully equipped
to be holy. Pause before responding to
people or situations, giving My Spirit space
to act through you.

Dear Jesus,

Holiness is one of those virtues that seems so elusive.
If I strive to be holy, I'm in danger of falling prey to
serious sins, especially pride and hypocrisy. Yet Your
Word clearly instructs me to be holy. I'm intrigued
by the idea that holiness is a matter of letting You live
through me. That seems more feasible than trying with
all my might to be good.

Beloved, be careful not to confuse *being* holy with
trying to *appear* holy. The Pharisees fell into that
trap: parading their pretension of holiness on street
corners, at banquets, in the temple—wherever they
found an audience. I reserved some of My strongest
condemnation for them and their hypocrisy.

When you became a Christian, I put the Holy
Spirit in you, thus equipping you to be holy. However,

you are still vulnerable to the world, the flesh (sinful nature), and the devil. These three conspire against holiness, tempting you to respond to people and situations in your old, habitual ways. My Spirit will not force His ways on you, so it's easy for you to ignore His inner Presence. That's why I encourage you to pause before responding—inviting the Spirit to live and love through you.

Remember that I am Christ in you, the hope of Glory. The more you know Me and love Me, the easier it is for you to let Me live through you. Without your even realizing it, intimacy with Me transforms you into My likeness—My holy image.

But just as he who called you is holy, so be holy in all you do;
for it is written: "Be holy, because I am holy."
1 Peter 1:15–16

You, however, are controlled not by the sinful nature but
by the Spirit, if the Spirit of God lives in you. And if anyone
does not have the Spirit of Christ, he does not belong to Christ.
Romans 8:9

To them God willed to make known what are the riches
of the glory of this mystery among the Gentiles:
which is Christ in you, the hope of glory.
Colossians 1:27 NKJV

I am everywhere at every time, ceaselessly working on your behalf. That is why your best coping strategies are trusting Me and living close to Me.

Dear Jesus,

You are indeed an awesome God! Who but You could be everywhere at every time? It amazes me that One so great as You would care about the many details of my life. Yet You do! When I ponder these glorious truths, I feel safe—knowing I am never alone. Help me, Lord, to keep these truths before me—to keep *You* always before me. Otherwise, I fall back into my default mode: straining and striving as if outcomes were totally up to me.

Beloved, I am pleased that you want to keep My very Presence before you—not just truths about Me. It's so easy for My children to confuse knowledge about Me with knowing Me experientially. The apostle Paul understood this distinction: He wrote about needing Power through My Spirit, to grasp the vast magnitude of My Love—Love that surpasses knowledge! Knowing Me is so much more than an activity of the mind.

You asked for help in keeping Me always before you. This is largely a matter of trusting Me. Sometimes you are keenly aware of My Presence; at other times, this awareness is minimal—or even absent. When you feel alone, you need to rely on your trust in Me. Continue to live and communicate as if I am with you, because I am! I have promised I will never leave you or forsake you. Instead of running after other gods when you feel needy, concentrate on coming nearer to Me. No matter what is happening, trusting Me and drawing close to Me are excellent strategies for living well.

I have set the LORD always before me.
Because he is at my right hand, I will not be shaken.
Psalm 16:8

I pray that out of his glorious riches he may strengthen you with power through his Spirit in your inner being, so that Christ may dwell in your hearts through faith. And I pray that you, being rooted and established in love, may have power, together with all the saints, to grasp how wide and long and high and deep is the love of Christ, and to know this love that surpasses knowledge— that you may be filled to the measure of all the fullness of God.
Ephesians 3:16–19

Keep your lives free from the love of money and be content with what you have, because God has said, "Never will I leave you; never will I forsake you."
Hebrews 13:5

Your awareness of your constant need
for Me is your greatest strength.
Your neediness, properly handled,
is a link to My Presence.

Dear Jesus,

I admit I would prefer to be less needy. On the
other hand, I do enjoy the closeness that comes from
consciously depending on You. It is so true that my
neediness must be properly handled. Otherwise, I'm
vulnerable to becoming anxious—or even angry—about
my situation. Help me accept my needy dependence as
a gift from You.

Beloved, I can read your thoughts all too well: I
know how much time you spend daydreaming
about getting beyond your needy condition. But there
is a better way. Instead of trying to figure out how to
escape problems in your life, use them to come closer
to Me. You need to remember—and believe—that My
way is perfect. I can use everything in believers' lives
for good, to the extent that they trust Me. One of the

most powerful ways to strengthen your trust in Me is to thank Me for the things that are troubling you. This expression of thankfulness will help you accept your neediness as a gift from Me.

The world has it all wrong about what constitutes success. Media (and even some churches) promote health and wealth as ultimate goals. But I have showered you with humble, rarely sought gifts: neediness and weaknesses. These gifts, properly received and used, help make My ways known on earth. Moreover, as you look up to Me in your neediness, My Face shines upon you—linking you to Me in radiant Joy.

As for God, his way is perfect; the word of the Lord is flawless.
He is a shield for all who take refuge in him.
2 Samuel 22:31

May God be gracious to us and bless us
and make his face shine upon us,
that your ways may be known on earth,
your salvation among all nations.
Psalm 67:1–2

Those who look to him are radiant;
their faces are never covered with shame.
Psalm 34:5

> In union with Me you are complete. In closeness to Me, you are transformed more and more into the one I designed you to be.

Dear Jesus,

I often feel incomplete, as if some vital part of me is missing. When this is just a feeling—not a conscious thought—I respond in many unproductive ways: foraging for food, looking for entertainment, searching for myself in the mirror, and so on. All the while, You are with me, patiently waiting for me to remember You. If I continue to go my own way—seeking satisfaction where there is none—I become increasingly frustrated. My agitated condition makes it hard for me to turn back to You, the only One who can complete me. I have found, though, that it is never too late to cry out, "Help me, Jesus!"

Beloved, when a child of Mine calls out to Me, I never fail to respond. I may not provide instant relief, as if I were just a genie, but I go to work immediately, setting in motion the conditions you need. I help you gain awareness of what you have been doing: seeking fulfillment in worldly ways. In response to your neediness, I offer you My glorious riches. When you have settled down enough to see clearly, I proffer Myself to you. I invite you to come near Me, where you can find completeness.

As you center your attention on Me, I draw closer to you. While you rest in the rarified air of My Presence, I bless you with My Peace. Though you are just a jar of clay, I fill you with My treasure: the Light of the knowledge of My Glory. This divine Light fills you to the brim—making you complete. It also transforms you, bit by bit, into the masterpiece I designed you to be.

Perseverance must finish its work so that you may
be mature and complete, not lacking anything.
James 1:4

He fulfills the desires of those who fear him;
he hears their cry and saves them.
Psalm 145:19

Submit yourselves, then, to God. Resist the devil, and he will flee
from you. Come near to God and he will come near to you.
James 4:7–8

For God, who said, "Let light shine out of darkness," made his light
shine in our hearts to give us the light of the knowledge of the glory
of God in the face of Christ. But we have this treasure in jars of clay to
show that this all-surpassing power is from God and not from us.
2 Corinthians 4:6–7

When you spend time with Me, I restore your sense of direction. I enable you to do less but accomplish more.

Dear Jesus,

This is good news indeed! What You are offering is just what I need. There are so many possible ways to go through each day that I easily lose my sense of direction. When this happens, I tend to go around in circles: interrupting one task to do something else, while my thoughts flit from one thing to the next. At such times my body simply cannot keep up with the pace of my mind, and I become increasingly confused—accomplishing little. I know my time and energy are precious gifts from You, Lord. Help me use them wisely.

Beloved, when you realize you have lost your way, there is only one remedy: Stop, and reconnect with Me—the Director of your life. Admit that you are directionless, and ask for My help. Pause with Me, while I soothe your frazzled nerves. Let the peacefulness of My Presence revive you. As My Peace settles over your mind and soul, the way before you will open up step by step. Though you cannot see very far ahead of you, you can see enough to continue your journey. Try to remain conscious of Me as you go, remembering that I am with you every bit of the way.

You may think this delay is a waste of time, but it is not. When you follow My directions closely, you save great quantities of time and energy: You avoid doing worthless works—things that are not in My plan for you. This frees you to do the genuine works I prepared in advance for you. Thus, though you do less in terms of actual activity, you accomplish much more.

Commit to the LORD whatever you do,
and your plans will succeed.
Proverbs 16:3

The LORD replied, "My Presence will
go with you, and I will give you rest."
Exodus 33:14

Direct me in the path of your commands, for there I find delight.
Psalm 119:35

For we are God's workmanship, created in Christ Jesus to do
good works, which God prepared in advance for us to do.
Ephesians 2:10

> Seek to please Me above all else.
> Let that goal be your focal point
> as you go through this day.

Dear Jesus,

I definitely need a focal point to guide me through this day. My mind slips out of focus very easily. When I fix my thoughts on You, the fog lifts and I can see things more clearly. A good way to stay focused on You is seeking to please You moment by moment. I really do want to please You, but I am easily sidetracked by lesser goals.

Beloved, you will not be able to achieve success through discipline alone. This pursuit requires much more than an act of your will: It is largely powered by what is in your heart. As your Love for Me grows stronger, so does your desire to please Me. When a man and a woman are deeply in love, they take great delight in pleasing one another. They may spend hours pondering ways to surprise their beloved with unexpected pleasures. Simply anticipating the loved one's happiness is exciting to such a lover. Actually, I Myself am such

a Lover. I delight in increasing your Joy: making it
complete. The best way to grow in your passion for Me
is to increase your awareness of My ardent Love for you.

Whenever you seek to please Me, think about
Me as the Lover of your soul: the One who loves you
perfectly every nanosecond of your existence. Let your
budding desire to please Me flourish in the Light of
My unfailing Love.

> Therefore, holy brothers, who share in the
> heavenly calling, fix your thoughts on Jesus,
> the apostle and high priest whom we confess.
> *Hebrews 3:1*

> As the Father has loved me, so have I loved you.
> Now remain in my love. If you obey my commands,
> you will remain in my love, just as I have obeyed my
> Father's commands and remain in his love. I have told
> you this so that my joy may be in you and that
> your joy may be complete.
> *John 15:9–11*

> But I am like an olive tree flourishing in the house of God;
> I trust in God's unfailing love for ever and ever.
> *Psalm 52:8*

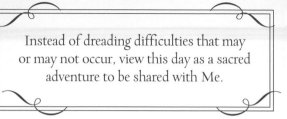

Instead of dreading difficulties that may or may not occur, view this day as a sacred adventure to be shared with Me.

Dear Jesus,

My heart delights in Your invitation to live this day as a sacred adventure. You are my King of kings, and I long to live in a manner that displays my adoption into Your royal family. You are also my Lord of lords, so anything shared with You is sacred. I admit, though, that my mind is often preoccupied with ordinary matters and concerns. When a new day stands open before me, I scan it for difficulties that may occur, wondering if I'll be able to cope. This is the natural bent of my mind: an earth-bound focus.

Beloved, it is natural for your mind to be drawn toward mundane matters. But you are capable of so much more than that! I created you in own My image, with incredible abilities given only to mankind. When you became a believer, I infused My Spirit into your innermost being. The combination of

My image and My Spirit in you is powerful—making you fit for greatness.

I want you to begin each day viewing yourself as a chosen warrior, ready to go into battle. Of course, there will be difficulties, but they need not be your focus. Put on the full armor I have provided, and you will be ready for whatever battles you have to fight. When you are engaged in combat, keep looking to Me for strength and guidance. Remember that you and I together can handle whatever difficulties come your way. Abandon yourself to the challenges I have chosen for you. Then you will find your days increasingly devoted to sacred adventures shared with Me—your King!

God, the blessed and only Ruler, the King of kings and Lord of lords, who alone is immortal and who lives in unapproachable light, whom no one has seen or can see. To him be honor and might forever. Amen.
1 Timothy 6:15–16

And if the Spirit of him who raised Jesus from the dead is living in you, he who raised Christ from the dead will also give life to your mortal bodies through his Spirit, who lives in you.
Romans 8:11

Therefore put on the full armor of God, so that when the day of evil comes, you may be able to stand your ground, and after you have done everything, to stand.
Ephesians 6:13

> Go gently through this day, leaning
> on Me and enjoying My Presence.

Dear Jesus,

Gently seems to be the only way I can make it through this day. I'm grateful for Your perfect understanding: for commanding me to do precisely what I need most at this moment. Thank You also for inviting me to lean on You. I need to lean on someone, and You are definitely the most reliable Person I could ever find. It amazes me that You—the Lord of the universe—are always available to help me.

Beloved, My availability is based on My commitment to you, which is deeper and stronger than even the most ardent wedding vows. No matter how passionately in love a bride and groom may be, their vows last only until one of them dies. My commitment, however, is absolutely unlimited. When you asked Me to be your Savior, I wed you for eternity. Neither death nor life, nor anything else in all creation can separate you from My Love!

I want you to go gently through this day, because I Myself am gentle—especially with those who are weak. You are free to lean on Me as much as you like, but I also want you to enjoy Me. When you are weary, you find it easier to lean on Me than to enjoy My company. In an attempt to save energy, you tend to shut down emotionally. But it is possible for you to be joyful in Me—Your Savior—even in desperate circumstances. Remember that I am your strength. Rejoice in Me, and relax while I speak to you in a gentle whisper.

For I am convinced that neither death nor life, neither angels nor demons, neither the present nor the future, nor any powers, neither height nor depth, nor anything else in all creation, will be able to separate us from the love of God that is in Christ Jesus our Lord.

Romans 8:38–39

Though the fig tree does not bud and there are no grapes on the vines, though the olive crop fails and the fields produce no food, though there are no sheep in the pen and no cattle in the stalls, yet I will rejoice in the LORD, I will be joyful in God my Savior. The Sovereign LORD is my strength; he makes my feet like the feet of a deer, he enables me to go on the heights.

Habakkuk 3:17–19

After the earthquake came a fire, but the LORD was not in the fire. And after the fire came a gentle whisper.

1 Kings 19:12

> I am nearer than you dare believe, closer than the air you breathe. If My children could only recognize My Presence, they would never feel lonely again.

Dear Jesus,

I deeply desire to experience Your Presence more consistently. When I am aware of Your nearness, I feel peaceful and content. It's awesome that You are even closer than the air I breathe. Usually, I'm not conscious of being enveloped in air, because it is invisible and constantly available to me. Similarly, Your unseen Presence is a constant in my life, but I often fail to recognize You. That leaves me vulnerable to loneliness.

Beloved, it's good that you see the connection between loneliness and lack of awareness. This is an age-old problem. When the patriarch Jacob was in a barren place—far from his family—he was quite conscious of his isolation. However, I poured out My Presence upon him, in the form of a glorious dream. When Jacob awoke, he responded, "Surely the LORD is in this place, and I was not aware of it" (Genesis 28:16).

It is possible to feel isolated even when you are with other people, because of the privacy of your thoughts and unspoken needs. The only thing that can adequately fill the gaps of isolation is awareness of My abiding Presence. Not only am I constantly with you, but I am also within you: in the inner recesses of your heart and mind. My knowledge of you is picture-perfect, and it is framed in unconditional Love.

Let feelings of loneliness remind you of your need to seek My Face. Come to Me with your ever-so-human emptiness, and My divine Presence will fill you with Life to the full!

In my integrity you uphold me and
set me in your presence forever.
Psalm 41:12

The LORD is righteous in all his ways and loving toward
all he has made. The LORD is near to all who call on him,
to all who call on him in truth.
Psalm 145:17–18

The thief comes only to steal and kill and destroy;
I have come that they may have life, and have it to the full.
John 10:10

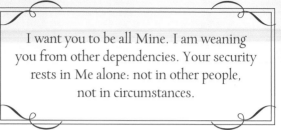

I want you to be all Mine. I am weaning you from other dependencies. Your security rests in Me alone: not in other people, not in circumstances.

Dear Jesus,

I'm grateful for the security You provide in my life. The world has become such a frightening, insecure place! If You were not my Savior, I don't know how I would cope with all the uncertainty. However, I am not yet weaned from other dependencies: I want to depend on You plus other people and favorable circumstances.

Beloved, I am pleased by your candid admission. That gives Me an entrance into your life, so I can work with you on this matter. I'm not asking you to become a hermit or otherwise isolate yourself from other people. On the contrary, I want My children to help and love one another. One of the main ways I bless people is through the loving acts of others. However, you need to remember that every good and perfect gift is ultimately from Me, even if it comes to you through human hands.

The main danger of misplaced dependence is that it can border on idolatry. If you let your basic well-being depend on another person's behavior, you elevate that one to a position that only I should occupy. This is not only displeasing to Me; it is destructive. Because people are imperfect and unpredictable, your life may come to resemble a roller-coaster ride: subject to the whims and moods of another person. Even worse, your intimacy with Me will be hindered by your preoccupation with someone else. I deserve first place in your heart!

I want you to rejoice in Me at all times, in all kinds of circumstances. You may ask freely for whatever you desire, bringing Me your petitions with thanksgiving. Regardless of how I answer your requests, this prayer-transaction comes with a promise: My Peace will guard your heart and your mind, keeping you close to Me.

Every good and perfect gift is from above,
coming down from the Father of the heavenly lights...
James 1:17

Yet I hold this against you: You have forsaken your first love.
Revelation 2:4

Rejoice in the Lord always... in everything, by prayer
and petition, with thanksgiving, present your requests to God.
And the peace of God, which transcends all understanding,
will guard your hearts and your minds in Christ Jesus.
Philippians 4:4–7

> Come to Me. Come to Me. Come to Me.
> This is My continual invitation to you,
> proclaimed in holy whispers.

Dear Jesus,

Your invitation makes my heart leap! How I long to hear Your holy whispers and respond with my whole being. So often, though, I'm distracted by the noise of my worries and the clamor of the world. Help me remember Your inviting Presence even when I'm too hassled to hear Your Love-whispers.

Beloved, you do well to ask for help in remembering. My chosen children have consistently forgotten Me and the great works I've done on their behalf. I made a dry path through the Red Sea for the Israelites, saving them from the pursuing Egyptians. Yet many of those former slaves remembered the tasty food they had eaten in Egypt better than they recalled My miraculous deeds to set them free. You also tend to "major on minors," letting trivial matters distract you from Me. You forget that My sacrificial death and miraculous resurrection shed Light on each moment of your life. I want you to live vibrantly in this Light, increasingly aware of My nearness.

To help in your endeavor to remember, think of Me as the Lover of your soul: the One who delights in you now and forevermore. View yourself first and foremost as My beloved, since that is your ultimate identity. Fill your mind with Bible verses that convince you of My perfect Love for you.

Come to Me at all times, My loved one. Pour out your heart to Me, for I am your Refuge.

Come to me, all you who are weary and burdened,
and I will give you rest.
Matthew 11:28

Then Moses stretched out his hand over the sea, and all that night the LORD drove the sea back with a strong east wind and turned it into dry land. The waters were divided, and the Israelites went through the sea on dry ground, with a wall of water on their right and on their left.
Exodus 14:21–22

Trust in him at all times, O people;
pour out your hearts to him, for God is our refuge.
Psalm 62:8

In addition to the three dimensions
of space and the one of time, there is
the dimension of openness to My Presence.
This one transcends the other four,
giving you glimpses of heaven while
you still reside on earth.

Dear Jesus,

I'm trying to wrap my mind around the concept of this fifth dimension—openness to Your Presence. It seems quite reasonable, because I know You transcend both space and time. However, I'm a time-bound creature: I can exist only in the present. Also, the world I see around me is decidedly three-dimensional. So, understanding this fifth dimension is a "stretch" for me—a stretch of faith.

Beloved,

you are right on target. Openness to My Presence is all about faith: believing that though I am invisible, I am both Real and really with you. This is foundational to knowing Me. However, there is also an art to knowing Me. It is very personal, because each of

My followers has a unique relationship with Me: comprised of all your communication with Me, your love for Me, your receptivity and responsiveness to Me.

Sometimes when you are seeking My Face, My Presence becomes more real to you than the space-time moment you occupy. The reality of My glorious Being outshines your current circumstances and lifts you above them. You feel free, and your spirit soars with Me. You rejoice in Me and are strengthened by that divine Joy. Thus, you enjoy glimpses of heaven while continuing to dwell on earth.

Now faith is being sure of what we hope
for and certain of what we do not see.
Hebrews 11:1

Then Jesus said, "Did I not tell you that
if you believed, you would see the glory of God?"
John 11:40

And God raised us up with Christ and seated us
with him in the heavenly realms in Christ Jesus.
Ephesians 2:6

Nehemiah said, "Do not grieve,
for the joy of the LORD is your strength."
Nehemiah 8:10

Trust Me in the midst of a messy day.
Your inner calm—your Peace in My
Presence—need not be shaken by
what is going on around you.

Dear Jesus,

Messy is a very apt description of this day. Many
things feel out of control, but I'm trying to trust You to
help me. My yearning to restore order in my little world
tends to give me an outward focus—on my circumstances.
I confess that my inner calm is easily shaken by what is
going on around me. I know Your Peace is still available
to me, but I'm having trouble accessing it.

*B*eloved, your honesty appeals to Me and draws
Me near you. When a messy day interrupts your
Peace, you discover that your sense of security is quite
dependent on circumstances. This is a very common
problem, and there are ways you can overcome it. The
best way is to stop what you are doing and seek My
assistance. Even a brief "time-out" from the confusion
is extremely beneficial. As you turn your attention to

Me, I help you see from My perspective. You realize you are not in the midst of an emergency, so you give yourself permission to slow down. This slower pace makes it easier to stay conscious of Me when you return to the messy situation.

Sometimes it is impossible for you to leave the situation even briefly. In this case, your challenge is to retreat to a place of inner calmness while your mind and body remain largely engaged in problem-solving. This is difficult, but it is still possible. Since I live in your heart, My Peace is accessible to you there. Ask Me to increase your awareness of My peaceful Presence. Keep returning your thoughts to Me, by whispering "Jesus." My Name is a strong tower; as you run to it, you know you are safe.

I have told you these things, so that in me you
may have peace. In this world you will have trouble.
But take heart! I have overcome the world.
John 16:33

My help comes from the LORD, the Maker of heaven and earth.
Psalm 121:2

The name of the LORD is a strong tower;
the righteous run to it and are safe.
Proverbs 18:10

> Be willing to go out on a limb with Me.
> If that is where I am leading you,
> it is the safest place to be.

Dear Jesus,

I'm really not much of a risk taker. I prefer to *play it safe*. However, staying close to You is my heartfelt desire. I want to follow wherever You lead—even if it's out on a limb. Help me follow You confidently, rather than fearfully.

Beloved, bring all your fears to Me. Fears that are not dealt with tend to magnify themselves. Expose them to the revealing Light of My Presence, and they will shrink to manageable proportions. Some of them may even become comical when you view them from this perspective.

As fearfulness loosens its grip on you, you are freed to follow Me. Grasp My hand tightly, as we edge our way out onto the limb. Since I go before you in this venture, you can keep your eyes on Me as you step out in faith. Soon we will get to a resting place, and then you can look around. If you like, glance back at the tree trunk: the place from which we branched out on this adventure. While gripping My hand to steady yourself, look toward the horizon; enjoy the view from this treetop perspective.

You are actually safer here—out on this limb with Me—than you would be on the ground. In this new, challenging environment you stay alert: communicating with Me continually, holding My hand in trusting dependence. Overly familiar surroundings may feel safer, but they can lull you into sleepy self-reliance. That is when you tend to forget about Me; it's also when you are most likely to fall. Follow Me confidently wherever I lead, and the shelter of My Presence will keep you safe.

If the LORD delights in a man's way, he makes his
steps firm; though he stumble, he will not fall,
for the LORD upholds him with his hand.
Psalm 37:23–24

Let us fix our eyes on Jesus, the author and perfecter of our faith,
who for the joy set before him endured the cross, scorning its
shame, and sat down at the right hand of the throne of God.
Hebrews 12:2

In the shelter of your presence you hide them from the intrigues of
men; in your dwelling you keep them safe from accusing tongues.
Psalm 31:20

A thankful attitude opens windows of heaven. Spiritual blessings fall freely onto you through those openings into eternity.

Dear Jesus,

I love the image of spiritual blessings falling upon me through heaven's open windows. And all You require of me is to be thankful! That seems such an easy condition; yet I stumble over it almost every day of my life. Help me overcome my ungrateful attitude.

Beloved, I rejoice in your desire to become more grateful. Throughout the Bible I repeatedly command thankfulness because it is vital to your well-being. It is also crucial for a healthy relationship with Me, since I am your Creator, your Savior, your King. When you thank Me, you acknowledge your indebtedness to Me: how much I have done for you. This attitude brings Joy both to you and to Me.

Giving thanks is similar to priming a pump with water so that it will produce more water. Since thankfulness is one of the spiritual blessings I bestow on you, it will increase along with the others when you "prime" Me with thanksgiving.

Remember that I am the God of all grace. When you fail in your endeavor to be thankful, simply ask Me for forgiveness. As you freely receive this priceless gift—remembering what it cost Me—your gratitude will grow. Look up to Me, and see spiritual blessings cascading down on you through wide-open windows of heaven.

Enter his gates with thanksgiving
and his courts with praise;
give thanks to him and praise his name.
Psalm 100:4

Blessed be the God and Father of our Lord Jesus Christ,
who has blessed us with every spiritual blessing
in the heavenly places in Christ.
Ephesians 1:3 NASB

Devote yourselves to prayer,
being watchful and thankful.
Colossians 4:2

Rejoice greatly, O daughter of Zion!
Shout, O daughter of Jerusalem!
Behold, your King is coming to you....

Zechariah 9:9 NKJV

> When you seek Me instead of the world's idols, you experience My Joy and Peace. These intangibles slake the thirst of your soul, providing deep satisfaction.

Dear Jesus,

My soul is often thirsty, even though I may not realize it at the time. I may think I'm just tired or bored or stressed out. So I start looking around in the visible world: searching for satisfaction, or at least some distraction. All the while, You are with me—invisible, yet infinitely Real. My soul thirsts for You, Jesus!

Beloved, the world offers more distractions than you could ever fit into one lifespan. They may provide some relief for a while, but your thirst for Me remains unquenched. When you realize that your deepest desire is for Me, you are well on the way to finding satisfaction. As you go along this path of Life, you will encounter companions I have chosen for you—Joy and Peace. Though they are intangible, their company is quite beneficial: They can relieve the thirst of your soul.

Joy is radiantly lovely. Her contagious laughter lifts you up and lightens your mood. Peace is quieter than Joy but equally attractive. Her serenity calms you, as you feel fully understood yet totally accepted. The longer you walk with these delightful companions, the better your journey will be. Moreover, Joy and Peace enhance your awareness of Me—the One who ultimately satisfies your soul-thirst.

I spread out my hands to you;
my soul thirsts for you like a parched land.
Psalm 143:6

As the deer pants for streams of water,
so my soul pants for you, O God.
My soul thirsts for God, for the living God.
When can I go and meet with God?
Psalm 42:1–2

You have made known to me the path of life;
you will fill me with joy in your presence,
with eternal pleasures at your right hand.
Psalm 16:11

Let the peace of Christ rule in your hearts, since
as members of one body you were called to peace....
Colossians 3:15

My Light shines most brightly through
believers who trust Me in the dark.
That kind of trust is supernatural:
a production of My indwelling Spirit.

Dear Jesus,

I love walking in the Light with You. I am a creature
who craves light—sunlight and even artificial light, but
especially the Light of Your holy Presence. I trust You
easily when there's plenty of light in my world. Trusting
You in the dark is another matter altogether; there's a
kind of desperation to it—clinging to You as if my life
depended on it.

Beloved, growing in grace is all about trusting
Me: in good times, in bad times, at all times. I
am Lord over all your circumstances, so I want to be
involved in every aspect of your life. One of the best
ways of connecting with Me—here and now—is trusting Me in the very situation where you find yourself.
When your world seems dark and you trust Me any-
way, My Light shines brightly through you. You may

not be aware of this illumination, but it is visible to many: both in heavenly realms and on earth. Your display of transcendent trust weakens spiritual forces of evil. People around you are strengthened and blessed by My supernatural Light showing through you.

Clinging to Me in the dark feels like an act requiring all your willpower. Exerting your will is definitely important, but there is more: My hand has an eternal grip on yours. I will never let go of you! Moreover, My indwelling Spirit empowers you to keep hanging on. When you feel on the brink of giving up, cry out for His assistance: "Help me, Holy Spirit!" This brief prayer enables you to tap into His vast Power. Be encouraged by knowing that though you may see only darkness, My Light is shining through you in surpassing splendor!

But if we walk in the light, as he is in the light,
we have fellowship with one another, and the
blood of Jesus, his Son, purifies us from all sin.
1 John 1:7

Trust in him at all times, O people;
pour out your hearts to him, for God is our refuge.
Psalm 62:8

Even there Your hand shall lead me,
And Your right hand shall hold me.
Psalm 139:10 NKJV

> The ultimate protection against sinking during life's storms is devoting time to develop your friendship with Me.

Dear Jesus,

I waste a lot of time worrying about storms I can see forming along the horizon of my life. Thankfully, many of them in the past have veered off in another direction: never reaching me. Some storms have actually hit, but usually they've lost much of their power by the time they get to me. I need to switch my focus from difficulties that *may* come my way to Your Presence, which is *always* with me.

Beloved, you will never find security by trying to anticipate all the storms that may reach you someday. Remember that I control the atmosphere of your life. Trust Me by relaxing and releasing your concerns into My capable care. It saddens Me to see you obsessing about possible problems, rather than bringing these matters to Me. When you find yourself anxiously scanning the horizon of your life, use that as a reminder to seek My Face. You will not find Me off in the distance. I am here beside you, nearer than you dare believe.

Instead of wasting time worrying, devote that time to developing close friendship with Me. Talk with Me about everything that concerns you—your pleasures as well as your problems. I am interested in everything that matters to you, because I am your perpetual Lover. Ask Me to lift your perspective from a problem-focus to a Presence-focus. Remember that I am holding you by your right hand. I guide you with My own counsel, based on eternal wisdom; so there's no need to worry about the future. When the time comes, I will personally escort you into Glory.

It is good for you to be near Me. Your best refuge in life's storms is close friendship with Me.

Look to the LORD and his strength; seek his face always.
1 Chronicles 16:11

I have loved you with an everlasting love;
I have drawn you with loving-kindness.
Jeremiah 31:3

Yet I am always with you; you hold me by my right hand.
You guide me with your counsel, and afterward you will take
me into glory.... But as for me, it is good to be near God. I have made
the Sovereign LORD my refuge; I will tell of all your deeds.
Psalm 73:23–24, 28

> Remember that your relationship with
> Me is saturated in grace. Therefore,
> nothing you do or don't do can
> separate you from My Presence.

Dear Jesus,

I am so thankful for Your grace. When I'm keenly aware of having failed You, I grasp on to grace for dear life. Feelings of guilt and fear conspire to convince me I have lost Your Love. My sense of unworthiness tempts me to punish myself for my sins. Then I remember You have clothed me with garments of salvation—arrayed me in Your own righteousness. My salvation is all about You and what You have done to rescue me. Help me feel more secure in Your Love.

Beloved, it is utterly impossible for Me to stop loving you. Your relationship with Me is so saturated in grace that the two are forever inseparable. Meat that has been marinated in a sauce cannot become unmarinated. The longer it soaks, the deeper the marinade penetrates: flavoring and tenderizing the meat. You have been soaking in grace ever since I became your Savior. The longer you "marinate," the more fully My grace permeates our relationship. It is impossible for you to become un-graced!

I want you to rest in the perfection of your salvation. My glorious grace makes you holy and blameless in My sight. So, nothing you do or fail to do could ever separate you from My Love.

For by grace you have been saved through faith...
Ephesians 2:8 NKJV

For I am convinced that neither death nor life, neither angels nor demons, neither the present nor the future, nor any powers, neither height nor depth, nor anything else in all creation, will be able to separate us from the love of God that is in Christ Jesus our Lord.
Romans 8:38–39

I delight greatly in the LORD; my soul rejoices in my God.
For he has clothed me with garments of salvation and arrayed me in a robe of righteousness.
Isaiah 61:10

For he chose us in him before the creation of the world to be holy and blameless in his sight. In love he predestined us to be adopted as his sons through Jesus Christ, in accordance with his pleasure and will—to the praise of his glorious grace, which he has freely given us in the One he loves.
Ephesians 1:4–6

Glorifying and enjoying Me is a higher priority than maintaining a tidy, structured life. Give up your striving to keep everything under control—an impossible task and a waste of precious energy.

Dear Jesus,

In my heart, glorifying and enjoying You is a much higher priority than maintaining order. In practice, however, I do strive to keep things under control. When that becomes my focus, I tend to lose sight of You. Even when I do think of You at such a time, I usually try to enlist Your help in restoring order. I want my life to display the deep desire in my heart: glorifying and enjoying You in carefree exuberance!

eloved, I delight in your heartfelt desire to "kick up your heels" in celebration of who I Am. I can see into the depths of your heart, and I know that what you have expressed is true. I also read your thoughts with perfect accuracy, so I realize how easily you lose sight of My Presence.

Let's think together about this problem. To glorify and enjoy Me as you desire, you need to relinquish control to Me. You may think this would involve giving up something precious, because controlling things is a way you try to feel secure. In reality, however, this effort is bound to fail. Even if you succeed in creating a tidy, structured life for a time, you will not be able to maintain it. So, what I'm asking you to give up—controllingness—is something that frustrates you far more than it helps you.

Instead of wasting your energy on an impossible task, endeavor to celebrate your relationship with Me. Learn to walk more consistently in the Light of My Presence. Indeed, those who walk in this Light can rejoice in Me all day long, exulting in My righteousness. Glorify Me by living joyously in My energizing Light.

I have brought you glory on earth by completing the work
you gave me to do. And now, Father, glorify me in your presence
with the glory I had with you before the world began.
John 17:4–5

O LORD, you have searched me and you know me. You know
when I sit and when I rise; you perceive my thoughts from afar.
Psalm 139:1–2

Blessed are those who have learned to acclaim you,
who walk in the light of your presence, O LORD. They rejoice
in your name all day long; they exult in your righteousness.
Psalm 89:15–16

Make Me your focal point as you move through this day. Just as a spinning ballerina must keep returning her eyes to a given point to maintain her balance, so you must keep returning your focus to Me.

Dear Jesus,

I definitely feel as if I've been spinning around today, but not like a graceful ballerina. Just when I'm about to regain my balance, another event surprises me and sets me spinning again. I find myself moving faster and faster, trying to keep up with everything that's going on around me. Only as I look to You in the midst of my circumstances can I find equilibrium.

Beloved, your only hope is to look to Me again and again and again. That's why I likened your situation to a ballerina who repeatedly finds her focal point as she twirls. Though many people think beginning the day with Me is sufficient, they frequently go off course unless they continue seeking Me throughout their waking hours. Learn from the ballerina: Each time she turns full circle, she returns her eyes to the same stationary point with a quick turn of her head. If she didn't do that, she would soon become very dizzy. Similarly, you need a stationary focus as you face the dizzying swirl of events in your life. Because I remain the same forever, I am your best focal point. To avoid losing your balance, you must keep looking to Me.

I realize you cannot fix your gaze on Me continually. I understand the limitations of your human condition: You will lose sight of Me at times. But because I am with you always, you can reorient yourself with a quick *glance* My way. The more frequently you return your attention to Me, the better balanced your life will be. This is how to fix your eyes on Me while living in a fallen world. I assure you, though, that in heaven your limitations will be lifted. Now you see as if you are looking in a mirror that gives only a dim, blurred reflection, but then you will see in reality—face to Face!

Let us fix our eyes on Jesus, the author and perfecter of our faith.
Hebrews 12:2

But you remain the same, and your years will never end.
Psalm 102:27

For now we see in a mirror, dimly, but then face to face.
1 Corinthians 13:12 NKJV

My deep desire is that you learn to depend on Me in every situation. I move heaven and earth to accomplish this purpose, but you must collaborate with Me in this training.

Dear Jesus,

I love depending on You—afterward! When the task before me is too challenging for me to handle confidently, I almost instinctively turn to You for help. These are times when I am painfully aware of my inadequacy: my need to depend on Someone far greater than I. They are scary moments—times of having to act on my belief that You will not let me down. These occasions of stepping out in faith feel very much like jumping off a cliff into open space, trusting You to catch me in mid-air. And You do! *That* is when I feel jubilant—after I've just experienced Your intervention: rescuing me and enabling me to accomplish things I could never do alone.

Beloved, it is good that you have experienced My intervening help many times. Had you refused to "jump off the cliff," you would not have had those thrilling experiences. I hope your feelings of fear will diminish as I prove My faithfulness to you time after time. Let Me suggest a technique that can help: When you face an event that unnerves you, take time to affirm your trust in Me—repeatedly, if need be. This takes your attention off yourself and your fear, helping you focus on Me and My great faithfulness.

Though I'm pleased by your willingness to depend on Me in tough situations, I desire much more from you. I want you to rely on Me even when you feel competent to handle a situation yourself. I have given you talents and abilities. When you utilize them, remember to do so thankfully, asking Me to help you use them wisely: according to My will. This collaborative way of doing things will not only help you accomplish more; it will also keep you close to Me— communing with Me, delighting in Me, enjoying Me.

I have strength for all things in Christ Who empowers me
[I am ready for anything and equal to anything through
Him Who infuses inner strength into me].
Philippians 4:13 AMP

Because of the LORD's great love we are not consumed,
for his compassions never fail. They are new every morning;
great is your faithfulness.
Lamentations 3:22–23

Quiet your mind in My Presence. Then you will be able to hear Me bestowing the resurrection blessing: "Peace be with you."

Dear Jesus,

Quieting my mind is quite a challenge. My thoughts tend to go off in many directions at once. I really want to hear Your benediction of Peace. Teach me how to slow down my thinking, so I can experience Your peaceful Presence more fully.

Beloved, you are already doing the most important thing: communicating with Me about your problem. It is also vital to find a place where you can sit quietly, letting your body relax. It's much easier to tone down your thinking when your body is still for a time, since mind and body are so intricately connected. As you slow down your breathing, you will find your thoughts becoming more manageable. This makes it possible to focus those thoughts on Me. While you do so, your entire being will become increasingly relaxed.

Ponder the wonder of My Presence with you. Refresh yourself in My promises: I will counsel you and watch over you. I will supply every need of yours according to My riches in Glory. Peace I leave with you; My Peace I give you.

Though My Peace is a forever-promise, you need frequent reminders. When your mind becomes quiet enough, listen for My resurrection blessing: "Peace be with you."

Jesus came and stood among them
and said, "Peace be with you!"
John 20:26

I will instruct you and teach you in the way you should go;
I will counsel you and watch over you.
Psalm 32:8

And my God will supply all your needs
according to His riches in glory in Christ Jesus.
Philippians 4:19 NASB

Peace I leave with you; my peace I give you.
I do not give to you as the world gives.
Do not let your hearts be troubled and do not be afraid.
John 14:27

> If you try to carry tomorrow's trouble today, you will stagger under the load and eventually fall flat. You must discipline yourself to live within the boundaries of today.

Dear Jesus,

This discipline is extremely difficult for me, but it is one I strongly desire to master. My focus slips from today into tomorrow with the greatest of ease. I'm beginning to realize this is a form of escapism. By focusing on tomorrow's problems, I avoid facing today's. However, this type of escapism is extremely unpleasant, since worry is so painful. Also, it's a way I sabotage myself: The more I worry about tomorrow, the less I can accomplish today.

Beloved, I agree with your self-analysis, but there is more. Focusing on tomorrow's trouble is not only escapist, it is also irresponsible. Each day of your life is a precious gift from Me. When you squander My gift, I am displeased. Of course, you cannot avoid thinking about tomorrow altogether. That, too, would be irresponsible. The real question is, where do you live most of the time—in the present or in the future?

I see all your thoughts, so I know how many of them are needlessly future-oriented. If you want to break this deeply ingrained habit, you will need to monitor your thinking relentlessly. It is helpful to pay attention to your feelings; they can give you clues that your thinking is off course. When your present surroundings are pleasant yet you start feeling some negative emotion, it's important to capture your thoughts and examine them. Most of the time you will discover you've been worrying about some future event. Offer that concern up to Me, asking Me to either take care of the matter Myself or help you deal with it later. Then, rejoice in Me: your Savior and Sovereign Lord. I enable you to go on the heights—transcending your trouble! (Habakkuk 3:19).

> Therefore do not worry about tomorrow, for tomorrow will worry about itself. Each day has enough trouble of its own.
> *Matthew 6:34*

> We demolish arguments and every pretension that sets itself up against the knowledge of God, and we take captive every thought to make it obedient to Christ.
> *2 Corinthians 10:5*

A life lived close to Me will
never be dull or predictable.
Expect each day to contain surprises!

Dear Jesus,

I seem to have a love-hate relationship with surprises. I enjoy the adrenalin rush that accompanies them; it wakes me up and takes me beyond my ordinary routine. However, there is also a part of me that longs for my life to be predictable. In fact, I usually try to arrange things so as to minimize the possibility of being startled. Nonetheless, I do want to live close to You. If nearness to You and surprises are a package deal, then I definitely choose the package.

Beloved, a life lived close to Me could never be predictable. My ways and thoughts are too high above yours for that to be possible. I will never limit Myself to doing only what you can anticipate and understand. To do so would be to cease being God! So, expect your life to become increasingly surprising as you grow closer to Me.

I want to help you become more joyful about your unpredictable journey with Me. There is actually much

merit in expecting each day to contain surprises. This
helps you view an unforeseen event not as something
wrong but as something from Me. With this mind-set
you are more likely to turn to Me immediately, rather
than getting upset. You can ask Me to help you find
all the good I have infused into the event. I also stand
ready to help you respond appropriately. If you feel
unsteady in the wake of a startling situation, simply
draw nearer to Me.

As you learn to expect surprises each day, your life
will become more exciting. You will discover traces of
My vibrant Presence in unusual places. Increasingly,
you will find your days bright with Joy—the pleasure of
knowing Me more intimately.

As the heavens are higher than the earth, so are my ways higher than
your ways and my thoughts than your thoughts.
Isaiah 55:9

With your help I can advance against a troop;
with my God I can scale a wall.
Psalm 18:29

And though you have not seen Him, you love Him, and
though you do not see Him now, but believe in Him, you
greatly rejoice with joy inexpressible and full of glory.
1 Peter 1:8 NASB

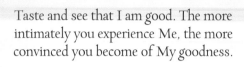

Taste and see that I am good. The more intimately you experience Me, the more convinced you become of My goodness.

Dear Jesus,

I have been taught since early childhood that You are good. However, that teaching did not change me significantly. Eventually I became a Christian, and I tasted Your goodness briefly. Yet I still did not know You very deeply. As a result, when things went badly in my life, I tended to resent Your ways with me. Only when I began investing time in seeking Your Face did I start to know You intimately. Now that I have tasted Your goodness, I want to experience more and more of You.

Beloved, your desire to know Me more fully is a delight to My heart. Actually, I have been pursuing you for quite some time. Long before you became a believer, I was working to reveal Myself to you. I placed experiences in your life that exposed your deep need to know Me. I brought you people in whom you could see the Light of My Presence. Even after you trusted Me as Savior I continued to pursue your heart, which was divided between Me and worldly goals. Finally, you began seeking Me with your whole heart, and I rejoiced!

Your wholeheartedness has opened the way for genuine intimacy between us. You have tasted My goodness, and you want more. I have responded to this desire in several ways: I've allowed suffering in your life, so that you can learn to trust Me more. Also, I have blessed you with intimate experiences of My Presence—to boost your confidence in My perfection. My goal is for you to become so convinced of My goodness that nothing can shake your trust in Me. Then, your soul will be deeply satisfied—as with the richest of foods.

Oh, taste and see that the LORD is good;
Blessed is the man who trusts in Him!
Psalm 34:8 NKJV

You will seek me and find me when
you seek me with all your heart.
Jeremiah 29:13

My soul will be satisfied as with the richest of foods....
Psalm 63:5

> Trust is like a staff you can lean on as you journey uphill with Me. If you trust in Me consistently, the staff will bear as much of your weight as needed.

Dear Jesus,

I find this teaching very comforting, since my journey seems to be more uphill than down. I love the idea of having something I can lean on as much as I need: a trust-staff. I confess there are many other things I tend to lean on in tough times, but not one of them is sufficient to bear the full weight of my neediness. Help me turn away from these inadequate supports and turn toward You—through trust.

*B*eloved, it's good that you want to turn away from your deficient supports. Not only will they let you down eventually, but they can become idolatrous. I'm delighted that you desire to turn toward Me through trust. If you want your trust-staff to support you adequately, you must lean on Me consistently. Don't wait till you're in desperate straits! Turn to Me before the mighty waters of trouble engulf you.

You said that more of your journey is uphill than down. That is as it should be. Ultimately, you are on a highway to heaven. Though there are many ups and downs along the way, the overall gradient is upward. I am in the process of transforming you—preparing you for an eternity of living face to Face with Me. Do not expect easy conditions on such a high-reaching adventure. But do expect Me to support you all the way to heaven. Lean on, trust, and be confident in Me with all your heart and mind!

> Lean on, trust in, and be confident in the Lord
> with all your heart and mind, and do not rely
> on your own insight or understanding.
> *Proverbs 3:5 AMP*

> Therefore let everyone who is godly
> pray to you while you may be found;
> surely when the mighty waters rise,
> they will not reach him.
> *Psalm 32:6*

> Then they returned … strengthening the disciples and encouraging
> them to remain true to the faith. "We must go through
> many hardships to enter the kingdom of God," they said.
> *Acts 14:21–22*

The Peace I give you transcends your intellect. When most of your mental energy goes into efforts to figure things out, you are unable to receive this glorious gift.

Dear Jesus,

I really desire to receive Your Peace. Yet I know I spend way too much time trying to figure things out. Actually, many of the problems I try to solve are not even my own. My overactive mind clamps on to other people's difficulties—trying to work out what the best solution might be. I'd like to think my motive is compassionate concern, but I know there is also a strong element of seeking to play god in people's lives. Help me relinquish this role, which was never meant to be mine, so I can rest in You—the One who has *everything* figured out.

Beloved,

your very active mind definitely causes you problems, but it can also be a source of blessing. You need to practice directing that mental energy toward Me. I have taught you to use My Name as a reminder that I am with you: Lovingly whispering "Jesus" can turn your day around. Giving thanks is another wonderful way to come into My Presence frequently. I also want you to use brief prayers of praise and petition, which glorify Me and soothe your anxious thoughts. None of this is new to you, but you need practice in these delightful disciplines.

If you use your mental energy to focus on Me, you will have no problem receiving My Peace. My Presence and Peace are inseparable: When your mind is stayed on Me, I keep you in perfect Peace. I understand that your ability to stay focused on Me is limited. I do not expect perfection from you—only perseverance. Never give up!

Do not be anxious about anything, but in everything,
by prayer and petition, with thanksgiving, present your
requests to God. And the peace of God, which transcends
all understanding, will guard your hearts
and your minds in Christ Jesus.
Philippians 4:6–7

A man's steps are directed by the LORD.
How then can anyone understand his own way?
Proverbs 20:24

You will keep him in perfect peace,
Whose mind is stayed on You,
Because he trusts in You.
Isaiah 26:3 NKJV

The more challenging your day, the more of My Power I place at your disposal. As your day, so shall your strength be.

Dear Jesus,

This is a wonderful, practical promise. My strength seems quite insufficient for the demands I face today. Yet I know Your promises are trustworthy and true. So I look to You for strength sufficient to handle the challenges of this day.

Beloved, no matter how inadequate you may feel, you can always look to Me for help. You don't need to go to a special place or assume a certain posture to seek My Face. Nor do you need to use elegant language or otherwise work to win My favor. I always look favorably on you, because I can see in you My own perfect righteousness. I am alive in you, and I know your thoughts better than you do. So a simple glance at Me, made in faith, is enough to connect you to My Power.

You tend to waste energy trying to determine whether your resources are adequate for the day's demands. How much better to simply acknowledge your inadequacy when you awaken each morning! This frees you to rely on My infinite sufficiency. If you stay in touch with Me throughout the day, I will place enough Power at your disposal to meet your needs as they arise.

You often run into trouble when you keep checking up on your "power gauge" rather than looking to Me for My provision. This self-assessment can lead to panic, which quickly sends you into a downward spiral. As your mind races, searching for ways to bolster your resources, you become increasingly anxious. Yet as soon as you turn away from self-help and turn toward Me— your ever-present Help—you find that your strength surges: becoming equal to the demands of your day.

Your sandals shall be iron and bronze;
As your days, so shall your strength be.
Deuteronomy 33:25 NKJV

Look to the LORD and his strength; seek his face always.
Psalm 105:4

God is our refuge and strength,
an ever-present help in trouble.
Psalm 46:1

Hope is a golden cord connecting you to heaven. This cord helps you hold your head up high, even when multiple trials are buffeting you.

Dear Jesus,

When my life is flowing smoothly, the golden cord of hope provides additional blessing—like icing on a cake. However, when I'm dealing with multiple trials, this cord is a lifeline protecting me from despair. As I cling to hope in the midst of trouble, I am able to perceive You cheering me on: encouraging me with the absolute certainty of heaven. In order to behold You, though, I have to keep my head held high. If it droops down, I lose sight of You and see only the perplexity of my problems.

Beloved, hope is indeed My gift to you in both good times and bad. I'm pleased that you rejoice in the promise of heaven even when your life is going smoothly. Many of My followers get so intent upon seeking pleasure in this world that they forget about their ultimate, eternal home.

It's good that you cling to My *hope-cord* as a lifeline when you're struggling with various problems. This reduces the weight of your burdens, making it easier for you to stand up straight. However, you must still make the effort to focus more on My Presence than on your difficulties. Your tendency to be problem-focused robs you of much Joy. As you cling to hope, looking to Me for help, you can be joyful and patient in the midst of affliction.

There is surely a future hope for you,
and your hope will not be cut off.
Proverbs 23:18

But since we belong to the day...putting on...
the hope of salvation as a helmet.
1 Thessalonians 5:8

Be joyful in hope, patient in
affliction, faithful in prayer.
Romans 12:12

We have this hope as an anchor for the soul, firm and secure.
It enters the inner sanctuary behind the curtain, where Jesus,
who went before us, has entered on our behalf.
Hebrews 6:19–20

Spend time allowing My Light to infuse your dreams with life, gradually transforming them into reality.

Dear Jesus,

I bring You my dreams. Some of them are shadowy and two-dimensional: lacking reality. Only You can breathe life into them. I'm tired of waiting, but the very nature of dreams is that they are beyond my control. So I wait in Your Presence, asking You to do what is impossible for me.

Beloved, someday you will realize this time of waiting is really a gift from Me. Whether or not your dreams come true, spending time in the Light of My Presence is extremely good for you. Consider the richness of sunlight: When it passes through a prism, you can see the seven distinct colors that are in it. Sunlight promotes growth and healing, and it has many other helpful qualities. However, the Light of My holy Presence is much more powerful and beneficial than natural light. That is why waiting on Me brings bountiful blessings. The full spectrum of My supernatural Light shines upon you while you linger in My Presence. Thus you receive many benefits: new strength, guidance, protection, encouragement, and countless other blessings.

Bring all your dreams into My vibrant Light, so we can look at them together. Some of them are not in My plans for you; as you commit them to Me, seeking My will, I gradually remove them from your heart. Other dreams I approve, encouraging you to work prayerfully toward reaching those goals. Some dreams, however, remain veiled in mystery. I neither remove them from your heart nor provide a path for you to follow. This keeps you waiting on Me, enjoying the benefits of My Presence. When time is right, I can transform your long-held hopes into delightful reality.

For with you is the fountain of life; in your light we see light.
Psalm 36:9

Though youths grow weary and tired, and vigorous young men
stumble badly, yet those who wait for the LORD will gain new
strength; they will mount up with wings like eagles...
Isaiah 40:30–31 NASB

Yet the LORD longs to be gracious to you; he rises to
show you compassion. Blessed are all who wait for him!
Isaiah 30:18

Come to Me when you are hurting, and
I will share your pain. Come to Me when
you are joyful, and I will share your Joy—
multiplying it many times over.

Dear Jesus,

I'm grateful that no matter what condition I'm in,
I can come to You—just as I am. I don't have to clean
up my act first, since You already know the worst about
me. When I'm hurting, I want to be with someone who
understands me without condemning me. When I'm
happy, I delight in being with someone who loves me
enough to celebrate with me. Help me bring more and
more of myself to You.

Beloved, this is a good request: better than you realize. Most people are selective about which parts
of themselves they bring to Me. Some hesitate to bring
traits they consider shameful. Others are so used to
living with painful feelings—loneliness, fear, guilt—that
it never occurs to them to ask for help in dealing with
these things. Still others get so preoccupied with their
struggles that they forget I'm even here.

There are hurting parts of you that I desire to heal. However, some of them have been with you so long that you consider them part of your identity. You carry them with you wherever you go, with little awareness. On occasions when you have brought some damaged portion of yourself to Me, I have helped you walk in newfound freedom. However, you are so addicted to certain painful patterns that you cannot easily break free from them. Only repeatedly exposing them to My healing Presence will bring you long-term freedom. When that happens, you will be released to experience Joy in much fuller measure. I will share your Joy and multiply it many times over.

Therefore, there is now no condemnation
for those who are in Christ Jesus.
Romans 8:1

The LORD has done great things for us,
and we are filled with joy.
Psalm 126:3

In my anguish I cried to the LORD,
and he answered by setting me free.
Psalm 118:5

> Remember that you live in a fallen world:
> an abnormal world tainted by sin. Much
> frustration and failure result from your
> seeking perfection in this life.

Dear Jesus,

I know I live in a fallen world, but sometimes I slip into denial of that truth. I'm still driven to seek perfection where it can never be found—this world. I waste so much time and energy trying to do things perfectly, when simply getting them done would be sufficient. This leads not only to frustration but also, at times, to its close ally: anger. Please help me break out of this self-defeating behavior.

Beloved, your yearning for perfection is not bad in itself. I placed this longing in your heart so you would search for Me. However, your heart also contains many effects of the Fall. As a result, you often seek perfection apart from Me. This sets you on a path of frustration and failure—sometimes even idolatry. You can always return to Me by choosing to seek Me first and foremost. As you do so, I set your feet on a rock and give you a firm place to stand. I also put a new song in your mouth: a hymn of praise.

Do not try to stifle your longing for perfection. It serves a paramount purpose—pointing you not only to Me but also to your future, eternal home. Your unsatisfied yearnings can awaken you to the radiant perfection awaiting you in heaven. So, let the frustration of living in a fallen world remind you that you originated in a perfect place (Eden) and you're on the way to an inexpressibly glorious place—heaven!

He lifted me out of the slimy pit, out of the mud and mire;
he set my feet on a rock and gave me a firm place to stand.
He put a new song in my mouth, a hymn of praise to our God.
Many will see and fear and put their trust in the LORD.
Psalm 40:2–3

Now the LORD God had planted a garden in the east, in Eden;
and there he put the man he had formed.
Genesis 2:8

But our citizenship is in heaven. And we eagerly await a Savior
from there, the Lord Jesus Christ, who, by the power that enables
him to bring everything under his control, will transform our
lowly bodies so that they will be like his glorious body.
Philippians 3:20–21

> Because you are human, you will always
> have ups and downs in your life experience.
> But the promise of My Presence limits how
> far down you can go.

Dear Jesus,

I have a hard time accepting the downs in my life. I tend to feel like a failure at such times. It comforts me to realize this is simply part of being human. When I'm really feeling *down*, it's almost impossible to remember the Joy of Your Presence. So when You are absent from my emotions, I cling to the promise of Your Presence.

Beloved, I assure you that I can bring much good out of the times in your life when you are sad. These painful times teach you to depend on Me more fully, as you seek My Face for help and strength. I have blessed you with many joyful experiences as well, but you must not cling to them or try to make them permanent. Rather, hold them lightly—with open hands—enjoying the beauty of the moment. Thank Me for what you are experiencing, and your gratitude will increase your Joy.

Be willing to release the pleasures to Me in due time; then move on to the next stage of your journey.

When Sorrow becomes your travel companion, embrace her as a blessing from Me. If you receive her into your heart, she will bring new depth and richness to your soul. She can teach you more about Me—a Man of sorrows, familiar with suffering. She can also give you hope, based on the promise of My Presence. Hoping in Me will limit how far down you go in your suffering; it assures you that you will *again praise Me for the help of My Presence*. Although this protects you from falling into deep despair, it is not a "quick fix." You and Sorrow may continue to journey together for a while. Nonetheless, you will discover along the way a new capacity growing within you: the ability to be *sorrowful, yet always rejoicing*.

He was despised and rejected by men, a man of sorrows, and familiar with suffering. Like one from whom men hide their faces he was despised, and we esteemed him not.
Isaiah 53:3

Why are you in despair, O my soul? And why have you become disturbed within me? Hope in God, for I shall again praise Him for the help of His presence.
Psalm 42:5 NASB

Sorrowful, yet always rejoicing....
2 Corinthians 6:10

> The secret of being thankful is learning to see everything from My perspective. My world is your classroom. *My Word is a lamp to your feet and a light for your path.*

Dear Jesus,

I know from experience that days when I'm thankful tend to be times of blessing. Sometimes it's easy to be grateful—when I wake up on the *right* side of the bed and encounter no major problems. At other times, thankfulness feels as unreachable as the stars. That's when I need a perspective-lift: helping me see things from Your viewpoint.

Beloved, I delight in lifting your perspective. That's why I ventured into your world as an infant, even though I knew the price I would pay. My motivation was to *open eyes that are blind, to free captives from prison, and to release from the dungeon those who sit in darkness.* When you are feeling thankless, ask Me to open your eyes and release you from the dark dungeon of ungratefulness.

You live in an age of entitlement, so you need to counteract the barrage of propaganda proclaiming you deserve more. One way to lean against such lies is to jot down each day some things for which you are thankful. This helps you focus on blessings in your life, rather than on things you want but do not have.

It is crucial to saturate your mind with Scripture: reading it, pondering it, memorizing portions of it. This can help you see things from My infinitely wise perspective. My Word is *sharper than any double-edged sword;* I use it to perform spiritual surgery on *the thoughts and attitudes of your heart.* As Scripture lights up your perspective and your path, I set you free from the prison of ingratitude. Thus I release you to enjoy the pleasures of a thankful heart.

To open eyes that are blind, to free captives from prison and
to release from the dungeon those who sit in darkness.
Isaiah 42:7

Your word is a lamp to my feet and a light for my path.
Psalm 119:105

For the word of God is living and active. Sharper than any
double-edged sword, it penetrates even to dividing soul and spirit,
joints and marrow; it judges the thoughts and attitudes of the heart.
Hebrews 4:12

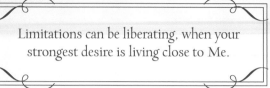

Limitations can be liberating, when your strongest desire is living close to Me.

Dear Jesus,

This is a fascinating concept. It seems almost paradoxical: Liberation is about becoming free, and limitations set boundaries around freedom. My desires bump up against such boundaries many times each day. I do want to live close to You, but I yearn for more freedom in my life.

Beloved, I know your limitations are hard to accept, but I also know how much good I can bring out of them. Many people are troubled by having too much freedom in their lives. This can have a paralyzing effect: They face so many possibilities that making decisions becomes extremely difficult. Your limitations actually provide a solid structure within which you can make choices about your life. Significantly, as you say yes to the boundaries I have placed around you, you can look up and see Me smiling upon you. You realize that *up* is the only direction where you face no limitations. What's more, you recognize that this is the most important dimension of your life.

Sometimes you feel cramped because you can't go very far to the right or the left, forward or backward, without bumping against a boundary. At such times you face an important choice: You can give in to feelings of frustration and self-pity, or you can look up to Me for help. If you choose Me, your limitations will give you wings. You can use those wings to soar heavenward, closer to Me. As you enjoy the heights in My Presence, glance down at the ground where your restrictions await you. From this perspective they look unimpressive—like lines drawn in the earth. Even when you return to ground level and your boundaries surround you again, you can look up to Me anytime. Bask in the Light of My smile, enjoying the easy intimacy of our relationship. Limitations can indeed be liberating, when your utmost desire is to live ever-so-near Me.

The LORD is close to the brokenhearted
and saves those who are crushed in spirit.
Psalm 34:18

And God raised us up with Christ and seated us
with him in the heavenly realms in Christ Jesus.
Ephesians 2:6

Now the Lord is the Spirit, and where the
Spirit of the Lord is, there is freedom.
2 Corinthians 3:17

Rejoice in this day of life, being willing
to follow wherever I lead. Follow Me
wholeheartedly, anticipating blessings
as we journey together.

Dear Jesus,

Since You have created this day of life and presented
it to me free of charge, help me receive it gratefully. My
natural tendency when I wake up is to assess the day
before me: trying to discern how good (or bad) it will
be. I do this almost unconsciously, often basing my
conclusions on something as trivial as the weather. I
would like to break free from this habit, so I can be more
receptive to You and Your blessings.

Beloved, I take much pleasure in your desire for
greater receptivity to Me. You have already
mentioned something that can help you in this quest:
a grateful attitude. If you awaken to find a dark, rainy
day, thank Me for the rain. Having done so, you will
be much less likely to grumble about the weather.
Also, remember that *I* have arranged the conditions

of your day. So you can assume there is much good to be found in it.

Rejoicing will help you find blessings in this day. If your circumstances are looking rather bleak, then be joyful in Me—your faithful Companion. Knowing how much I gave to rescue you from sin, you can trust that I have placed precious gifts along the path we are following. In faith, be on the lookout for good things—both great and small. Because I am your Teacher, I promise to provide learning opportunities as we travel together. When you reach the end of this day, stop and look back at the distance we have covered. Take time to ponder what you have learned and to savor the gifts you have found. Let your mind dwell on these things as you lie down to sleep, rejoicing in Me and My blessings.

This is the day the LORD has made; let us rejoice and be glad in it.
Psalm 118:24

"You call me 'Teacher' and 'Lord,' and rightly so, for that is what I am."
John 13:13

He who did not spare his own Son but gave him up for us all—how will he not also, along with him, graciously give us all things?
Romans 8:32

> The true question is not whether you can cope with whatever happens but whether you and I together can handle anything that occurs. It is this you-and-I-together factor that gives you confidence to face the day cheerfully.

Dear Jesus,

I really want to live this day confidently and cheerfully. That seems only fitting, since I am one of Your followers. But I often begin the day wondering how demanding it will be and whether I'll be able to cope. *Help me in my unbelief!*

Beloved, come to Me in your state of unbelief. I want you to experience My loving you perfectly even when your faith seems weak. Many of My followers wake up in a foggy, frazzled state of mind—as you do. However, I can see into your heart, where I find genuine trust in Me. Your challenge each morning is to untangle your thoughts so that they line up with the faith in your heart. You need to set aside adequate time each morning for this vital task. I want you to stay in My Presence—reading Scripture, praying, meditating on Me—till your mind is clear.

When you begin the day with a muddled mind, you tend to ask yourself the wrong question: whether you will be able to cope with whatever happens. But the true question is whether you and I together can handle the circumstances you face. As you look forward into the day, broaden your perspective so you can "see" Me there alongside you—strengthening, guiding, and encouraging you. If you omit this you-and-I-together factor from your perspective, you miss out on the help I am offering. So, as you work to unscramble your thinking, focus on who I am: *Immanuel—God with you*. While you meditate on this joyous focus, the qualms you had about the day will gradually give way to cheerful confidence.

I can do everything through him who gives me strength.
Philippians 4:13

He will have no fear of bad news;
his heart is steadfast, trusting in the LORD.
Psalm 112:7

"The virgin will be with child and will give birth to a son,
and they will call him Immanuel"—which means, "God with us."
Matthew 1:23

> I guarantee you will always have problems in your life, but they must not become your focus. When you feel yourself sinking in the sea of circumstances, cry out: "Help me, Jesus!" and I will draw you back to Me.

Dear Jesus,

Guarantees are usually about something positive, but this one (about constant problems) has a negative feel to it. It reminds me of a parent saying to a wailing child, "If you keep on crying, I'll give you something to cry about!" However, I know You well enough to trust that Your motive is not to threaten me but to help me.

Beloved, I do indeed want to help you deal with the problems in your life. There are a variety of wrong ways to handle difficulties: Some people simply pretend they don't exist—like ostriches hiding their heads in the sand. You, however, tend to go to the other extreme: You focus on problems much more than necessary. When you give in to this tendency, you become anxious and disheartened. I am training you to pry your mind away from trouble, so you can fix your thoughts on Me.

You are making progress, but you need to persevere in directing wayward thoughts toward Me.

One of the most challenging situations is when you are faced with many difficulties at the same time. You start to feel overwhelmed as your mind goes into high gear, trying to take care of everything at once. Your thoughts play hopscotch—jumping from one problem to the next, then turning around and jumping back again. If this continues too long, you become exhausted and begin to sink in the swirling sea of your circumstances. At this point, your emotional pain will alert you to your need for help. In a split second you can cry out: "Help me, Jesus!" and I will come to your rescue. As I pull you away from your problems, I draw you close to Me. While you gaze at Me, your panic begins to subside and you regain some sense of security. As you take time to enjoy My Presence, I bless you with My Peace.

Therefore...fix your thoughts on Jesus....
Hebrews 3:1

The LORD is near to all who call on him,
to all who call on him in truth.
Psalm 145:18

For He Himself is our peace....
Ephesians 2:14 NKJV

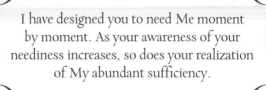

I have designed you to need Me moment by moment. As your awareness of your neediness increases, so does your realization of My abundant sufficiency.

Dear Jesus,

The longer I live, the more aware I become of my neediness. Many people—as they gain life experience—seem to become increasingly confident about the accuracy of their opinions. I, on the other hand, am increasingly aware that my understanding is like the tip of an iceberg: What I don't comprehend is so much greater than what I actually understand. This is just one of many areas where my neediness has become more apparent to me.

Beloved, recognizing the limits of your understanding is good, because it can enhance your relationship with Me. You need Me continually—not only for daily bread and blessings, but also for the myriad decisions you must make each day. If you had greater confidence in your knowledge and opinions, you might feel more comfortable. But walking close to Me on the path of Life is far more important than comfort. Remember that the road leading to Life is a narrow one, and only a few find it. So don't expect your journey along this path to be easy.

Awareness of your neediness helps you receive many blessings from Me. As you come to Me with your vast insufficiency, I draw near you with My infinite sufficiency. My abundant supply and your needy condition fit together perfectly—keeping you intimately connected to Me. The more consistently you rely on Me, the better your life will be. Not only will I meet all your needs through My glorious riches, I will also delight you with the Joy of My Presence. This is the way I want you to live: in joyful dependence on Me!

And my God shall supply all your needs according
to His riches in glory by Christ Jesus.
Philippians 4:19 NKJV

Enter through the narrow gate. For wide is the gate and
broad is the road that leads to destruction, and many enter
through it. But small is the gate and narrow the road
that leads to life, and only a few find it.
Matthew 7:13–14

Then will I go to the altar of God, to God, my joy and my delight.
Psalm 43:4

As you spend time in My Presence,
My thoughts gradually form in your mind.
My Spirit is the Director of this process.

Dear Jesus,

There are so many influences on my mind! I'm thankful for Your Spirit, who infuses Life and Peace into my mind. If I didn't have the Spirit's help, my thoughts would be savagely roaming the landscape of my brain— searching for satisfaction. Even so, my thinking is often unruly. I long to think Your thoughts more and more.

Beloved, I know even better than you the contents of your thoughts. Your mind is a spiritual battlefield. That's why I urge you to stay alert! When you spend time listening to Me, you need to begin with prayer for protection. The evil one is *the father of lies*; his deceptions can worm their way into your mind if you let down your guard. When you ask for protection, always pray in My Name, because I defeated the devil utterly on the cross!

I'm pleased that you desire to think My thoughts. Having prayed for protection, you should also ask the Holy Spirit to help you listen well. He is the Director of this listening adventure. Remain alert while you listen, ready to reject anything inconsistent with biblical truth. As My thoughts gradually form in your mind, you may find it helpful to write them down. Thank Me for what you have received, and continue to seek the help of My Spirit. Don't become overly focused on writing. The process—listening to Me under the direction of My Spirit—is more precious than the product: what you write. As you spend time focusing on Me, you will grow not only closer to Me but also more like Me.

The mind of sinful man is death,
but the mind controlled by the Spirit is life and peace.
Romans 8:6

Be self-controlled and alert. Your enemy the devil prowls
around like a roaring lion looking for someone to devour.
1 Peter 5:8

He [the devil] was a murderer from the beginning, not holding
to the truth, for there is no truth in him. When he lies, he speaks
his native language, for he is a liar and the father of lies.
John 8:44

> Walk with Me in holy trust, responding
> to My initiatives rather than trying to
> make things fit your plans.

Dear Jesus,

Thank You for making crystal-clear the choice I face many times each day: responding to Your initiatives in my life versus trying to force things into my plans. When I choose responsiveness, I gain closeness to You and ready access to Your resources. When I try to make things fit into my plans, I usually become frustrated and anxious. In spite of these negative consequences, however, I continue to feel a magnetic pull toward the planning path. This sabotages my deep desire to walk in Your ways, responding wholeheartedly to what You have prepared.

Beloved, I am blessed by your longing to walk in My ways, even when your behavior doesn't line up with that desire. This is really an issue of trust. There is nothing wrong with making plans, but you must not trust in them more than in Me.

I am calling you to walk with Me in holy trust. "Holy" means "set apart for sacred use." Your primary purpose in this life is to be available for sacred use: ready to do My will. When you get so focused on your plans that you hardly see anything else, you are unavailable to Me. If you start feeling frustrated or distant from Me, take time to seek My Face. Open yourself to My loving Presence. The magnetic attraction of My Love will empower you to resist the pull of your planning path. This frees you to respond to My initiatives: joining in the things I have already set in motion. For you are My own handiwork, born anew to do those good works I planned beforehand for you—taking paths I prepared ahead of time. Thus you live the good life that I prearranged and made ready for you.

In his heart a man plans his course,
but the LORD determines his steps.
Proverbs 16:9

The LORD is good, a refuge in times of trouble.
He cares for those who trust in him.
Nahum 1:7

For we are God's [own] handiwork (His workmanship), recreated in Christ Jesus, [born anew] that we may do those good works which God predestined (planned beforehand) for us [taking paths which He prepared ahead of time], that we should walk in them [living the good life which He prearranged and made ready for us to live].
Ephesians 2:10 AMP

> Instead of gazing into the unknown future,
> live each moment in joyful awareness of My
> Presence. I hold your future safely in My
> hands. It will unfurl before you as you go
> step by step through each day.

Dear Jesus,

I love this imagery. It reminds me of seeing red carpet rolled out in front of an honored person. I'm blessed by knowing that You hold my future safely in Your hands: releasing it to me moment by moment. Help me enjoy the wonder of Your Presence—accessible to me only in the present.

Beloved, I want to teach you how to spend more of your time in the present. The future, as most people conceptualize it, does not really exist. I hold it far beyond the reach of any person. When you or others gaze into the future, making predictions, you are simply exercising your imaginations. I alone have access to what is "not yet," because My existence isn't limited by time. As you go step by step through each day, I unroll the future before you. While you walk forward on the *red carpet* of time, you never set foot on anything but the present moment. Recognizing the futility of future-gazing can help set you free to live more fully in the present. The freer you become, the more you can enjoy the reality of My Presence.

Becoming free is a demanding process, because your mind is accustomed to wandering into the future at will. When you find yourself engaged in such thoughts, recognize that you are roaming in a fantasy land. As you awaken yourself with this truth, it's as if the ground drops out from under whatever you were fantasizing. This helps you return to the present: the here and now. I eagerly await you, ready to enfold you in My unfailing Love.

Since no man knows the future,
who can tell him what is to come?
Ecclesiastes 8:7

"I am the Alpha and the Omega," says the Lord God,
"who is, and who was, and who is to come, the Almighty."
Revelation 1:8

The LORD's unfailing love surrounds
the man who trusts in him.
Psalm 32:10

> Living close to Me is a way of continual newness. I, the Creator of the universe, am more creative than you can imagine.

Dear Jesus,

I love living close to You: It satisfies deep longings in me. I confess, though, that I'm a creature of habit. When I find a way of approaching You that works, I stick with that method—making it part of my routine. As I discover other means of drawing near to You, I add them to my routine as well. This approach helps me to be faithful in praying, but it is definitely not a way of continual newness. I would like to be more creative in my relationship with You, yet I don't want to abandon my old ways completely.

Beloved, your desire to live close to Me delights My heart. I'm also pleased that you are committed to praying for people and situations on a regular basis. I understand the tension you feel between being faithful in your prayers and being creative. Because your mind is both fallen and finite, you are not capable of continual creativity. Your routine prayers help you cover a wide range of praises and petitions without overtaxing your brain. But that very efficiency carries with it a danger: You can sleepwalk through your regular prayers. To avoid doing that, make use of the massive Power source within you—the Holy Spirit. He will help you stay alert, as you invite Him to empower your prayers with Life.

I'm not asking you to abandon your old ways of praying, but I *am* challenging you to seek new ways of communing with Me. You are capable of much more creativity than you realize, because I made you in My own image and put My Spirit within you. As you ponder ways to bring Me pleasure, I "tiptoe" closer to you. If you listen attentively, I will whisper some ideas in your mind. Seeking fresh ways to commune with Me will awaken your soul and enliven your relationship with Me.

In the beginning God created the heavens and the earth.
Genesis 1:1

And pray in the Spirit on all occasions with all kinds of prayers
and requests. With this in mind, be alert and always
keep on praying for all the saints.
Ephesians 6:18

For great is your love, reaching to the heavens; your faithfulness
reaches to the skies. Be exalted, O God, above the heavens;
let your glory be over all the earth.
Psalm 57:10–11

> Do not fear My will, for through it
> I accomplish what is best for you.
> Take a deep breath, and dive into the
> depths of absolute trust in Me.

Dear Jesus,

Although I often pray for Your will to be done, at times I'm fearful of what this may involve. I know that Your will sometimes includes pain. When I'm hurting—physically, emotionally, spiritually—I search for ways to relieve or escape my pain. This easily becomes my focus, as I obsess about how to solve my problems. Help me really believe that *Your way is perfect*.

*B*eloved, this is a good request, but the answer will not be easy. It is natural that you want to minimize pain. However, natural responses are often not the best. In My Word I continually call you to transcendent living: going beyond what is natural to what is supernatural. My will is far deeper than your understanding. Though My ways may entail sacrifice and pain, I accomplish through them not just what is good for you—but what is best.

Beneath the surface of this life—completely beyond your awareness—there are countless interconnections of people and events. Things that appear senseless to you make perfect sense when you can view the total picture. Occasionally I may give My followers glimpses of the big picture, to strengthen and encourage them. Generally, though, I call My people to *live by faith, not by sight*. Sometimes that will be frightening: like diving into water so deep that it seems bottomless. You need utter trust in Me to push through your fear into those unknown depths. After diving in, though, your buoyant body will gradually rise to the surface. You keep swimming till you're exhausted. When you can go on no longer, you begin to sink. However, just before your head goes under, your feet touch something solid! You realize My hands are beneath your feet. *I am your Refuge and dwelling place; underneath are the everlasting arms.*

As for God, his way is perfect…He is
a shield for all who take refuge in him.
2 Samuel 22:31

We live by faith, not by sight.
2 Corinthians 5:7

The eternal God is your refuge and dwelling place,
and underneath are the everlasting arms.
Deuteronomy 33:27 AMP

> While you wait in My Presence, I do My best work within you: transforming you by the renewing of your mind. Do not skimp on this vital time with Me.

Dear Jesus,

When there is work staring me in the face, it's a challenge to wait in Your Presence. My eager, active mind wants to plunge into the day's duties so that I can scratch them off my to-do list. I struggle to remember that Your work is more important than mine; I need to give You time to transform me.

Beloved, consider the work I am doing in you. Among other things, I am renovating your mind—a big job! As I shine the Light of My Presence into your mind, darkness flees and deception is unmasked. However, there are many crevices in your brain: places where old thought patterns tend to hide. My Spirit within you can search out and destroy those enemies, but He awaits your cooperation. Perhaps you consider waiting in My Presence a passive use of time, but it actually requires a lot of effort. Habitual ways of thinking do not die easily. When the Spirit shines His light on a hurtful thought pattern, you need to capture it by writing it down. Then bring it to Me, so we can examine it together. I will help you find the distortions and replace them with biblical truth.

The more you focus on Me and My Word, the more you can break free from distorted thoughts. Most of the distortions stem from childhood or from traumatic experiences you have endured. So the patterns are deeply etched into your brain. You may need to recapture the same thought many times before you gain mastery over it. But all that effort leads to a marvelous result: increased freedom to think My thoughts and commune deeply with Me. Wait with Me while I renovate you—from the inside out!

I wait for the LORD, my soul waits, and in his word I put my hope.
Psalm 130:5

Do not conform any longer to the pattern of this world,
but be transformed by the renewing of your mind.
Romans 12:2

We take captive every thought to make it obedient to Christ.
2 Corinthians 10:5

When you walk through a day with
childlike delight, savoring every blessing,
you proclaim your trust in Me:
your ever-present Shepherd.

Dear Jesus,

I would love to go through my days with childlike
delight—enjoying every blessing You provide. However,
I am rarely that lighthearted. Oh, I have my moments:
times when I rejoice in You and with You. I long for those
bright moments, which punctuate the timeline of my
days, to spread out and cover increasingly more of my life.

Beloved, this is a good desire, but you cannot
achieve it through self-discipline or by trying harder. Your ability to rejoice in Me with childlike delight
flows out of your relationship with Me. Think of all
it means to have Me as your Shepherd: My full-time
job is watching over you, taking care of you. Because I
am infinite, I can care for you as if you were My only
"sheep." Remember that I am the Good Shepherd.
When danger threatens, I never abandon you. I have

even gone so far as to lay down My Life for you. I, the Good Shepherd, know My sheep and My sheep know Me—just as the Father knows Me and I know the Father. Chew on that awesome truth as you lie down and rest in green pastures.

To walk through a day with carefree delight, you must trust in My Love with childlike certainty. Though the mountains be shaken and the hills be removed, yet My unfailing Love for you will not be shaken. The more you trust in this unfailing Love, the more you can enjoy My Presence. Look trustingly to Me while we journey together, and I will point out delights along the way. As you savor these pleasures, your bright moments will multiply in the Light of My Presence.

The LORD is my shepherd, I shall not be in want. He makes me lie down in green pastures, he leads me beside quiet waters.
Psalm 23:1–2

I am the good shepherd; I know my sheep and my sheep know me—just as the Father knows me and I know the Father—and I lay down my life for the sheep.
John 10:14–15

"Though the mountains be shaken and the hills be removed, yet my unfailing love for you will not be shaken nor my covenant of peace be removed," says the LORD, who has compassion on you.
Isaiah 54:10

> Human weakness, consecrated to Me,
> is like a magnet—drawing My Power
> into your weakness.

Dear Jesus,

This is good news! I have plenty of weakness to bring You. I've suspected for some time that my weaknesses are more useful to You than my strengths. Please teach me how to consecrate all of myself to You.

Beloved, this is a courageous request. Consecrating yourself to Me involves abandoning yourself to My service and worship. You relinquish to Me all rights of control over your life. When you consecrate weaknesses to Me, you are inviting Me to use them as I will—for My Glory and purposes. This requires vulnerability on your part: willingness to let lowly aspects of yourself be exposed to public scrutiny. Since this goes against the grain of human nature, you may need to dedicate yourself to Me day after day.

Though consecrating yourself to Me is costly, the benefits far outweigh the cost. As you release your weaknesses to Me for My purposes, you become a treasure in My kingdom. Making yourself fully available to Me guarantees that your life will not be wasted: I will use it for My Glory! When you offer your frailty to Me for My service, I receive it as a sacred act of worship. In response, I dispatch My Power to you. *My strength is fulfilled and completed—shows itself most effective—in your weakness.* Moreover, as you abandon yourself to Me, *My Power pitches a tent over you and dwells with you* (2 Corinthians 12:9 AMP).

I appeal to you therefore, brethren, and beg of you in view of [all] the mercies of God, to make a decisive dedication of your bodies [presenting all your members and faculties] as a living sacrifice, holy (devoted, consecrated) and well pleasing to God, which is your reasonable (rational, intelligent) service and spiritual worship.

Romans 12:1 AMP

Consecrate yourselves and be holy,
because I am the LORD your God.

Leviticus 20:7

You are worthy, our Lord and God, to receive glory and honor and power, for you created all things, and by your will they were created and have their being.

Revelation 4:11

> I have awakened in your heart strong desire
> to know Me. This longing originated in Me,
> though it now burns brightly in you.

Dear Jesus,

Thank You for awakening my heart! Before I knew
You, I tried to find life in many different places.
Often I would think I had found what I was searching
for—only to be disappointed later. After I became
thoroughly disillusioned, You reached down and took
me into Your own family. Years later, I began thirsting
for You: longing to know You at a deeper heart level.
I set aside time to meet with You as my living God—
vibrantly present with me.

Beloved, when you set out to know Me more
intimately, I rejoiced but I wasn't surprised. I had
been pursuing you long before you began your quest. I
was working in your life experiences, as well as in your
heart, mind, and spirit. Your desire for a closer walk with
Me grew out of My painstaking work in you. I initiated
your longing for Me, and your response delights Me.

It is important for you to know Me as the Initiator in our relationship. If you think it is your spiritual disciplines that keep you close to Me, you are at risk. Some days you may skimp on your time with Me or not be able to concentrate well. If you're depending on your own efforts to stay near Me, you will feel distant from Me at such times. But if you are relying on Me—what I have done, am doing, will do—you know My Love for you is always assured. So you can rest in Me: trusting in My unfailing Love, flourishing in My abiding Presence.

Above all else, guard your heart, for it is the wellspring of life.
Proverbs 4:23

My soul thirsts for God, for the living God.
When can I go and meet with God?
Psalm 42:2

I am the vine, you are the branches; he who abides in Me, and I in him, he bears much fruit, for apart from Me you can do nothing.
John 15:5 NASB

But I am like an olive tree flourishing in the house of God;
I trust in God's unfailing love for ever and ever.
Psalm 52:8

Anxious thoughts meander about and crisscross in your brain, but trusting Me brings you directly into My Presence.

Dear Jesus,

My thoughts do meander quite a bit, and they get tangled up with various thought fragments. It takes a lot of effort for me to *think straight*, especially when I'm anxious. Sometimes when I'm feeling frazzled, I say out loud or in a whisper: "I trust You, Jesus." This calms me down and helps me think more clearly.

Beloved, you have found an excellent way to calm yourself. That short statement switches your focus from you and your worries to Me and My boundless resources. Your affirmation of trust helps you remember that I am taking care of you; it also draws you closer to Me. As you commune with Me face to Face, you are free to express all your concerns. Some worries will evaporate as soon as you look at them in the strong Light of My Presence.

Other concerns remain, but you feel less anxious about them. Trusting Me to help you deal with those problems encourages you and gives you hope.

Remember that I am your Refuge: an unshakable fortress. Demonstrate your trust by pouring out your heart to Me—expressing all the feelings welling up inside you. I am your ever-present Helper: in good times, in bad times, at all times. Your soul finds rest in Me alone.

When I am afraid, I will trust in you.
Psalm 56:3

Then you will call upon Me and go and
pray to Me, and I will listen to you.
Jeremiah 29:12 NKJV

God is our refuge and strength, an ever-present help in trouble.
Psalm 46:1

Find rest, O my soul, in God alone; my hope comes from him.
He alone is my rock and my salvation; he is my fortress,
I will not be shaken. My salvation and my honor depend on God;
he is my mighty rock, my refuge. Trust in him at all times,
O people; pour out your hearts to him, for God is our refuge.
Psalm 62:5–8

Listen to Me even while you are listening
to other people. As they open their souls
to your scrutiny, you are on holy ground.
You need the help of My Spirit
to respond appropriately.

Dear Jesus,

This is an area where I really want to grow. When
people open up to me, I get so focused on them and
what they're saying that I forget to listen to You. The
latent hero in me tries to take charge of the situation and
rescue the other person. While I'm listening, my mind is
analyzing data: searching for solutions. The main problem
with this approach is that I'm relying on myself—trusting
in my own abilities, which are totally inadequate.

Beloved, it's good that you recognize your tendency
to play the hero. It's even better that you want to
grow out of this role. When people bare their souls to
you, you are indeed on holy ground. Your responsibility
is to listen and love. If you jump in with both feet—
trying to rescue them—your muddy footprints pollute
the holy terrain. Some people will retreat when this

happens; others may be too wounded to realize they've been violated. Either way, you have missed the mark and spoiled a splendid opportunity.

To function effectively on holy ground, you need the help of the Holy Spirit. Ask Him to think through you, listen through you, love through you. As the Spirit's Love shines through you, My healing Presence goes to work in the other person. While you continue listening, I will sometimes give you words of wisdom to share. But your main role is to direct the person toward Me and My limitless resources.

If you follow these guidelines, both you and others will be blessed. They will connect with My unfailing Love at soul-level. My Spirit will flow through you delightfully—refreshing your soul. You may not feel heroic, but your soul will feel satisfied.

"Do not come any closer," God said. "Take off your sandals,
for the place where you are standing is holy ground."
Exodus 3:5

Let the morning bring me word of your unfailing love,
for I have put my trust in you. Show me the way
I should go, for to you I lift up my soul.
Psalm 143:8

My soul will be satisfied as with the richest of foods....
Psalm 63:5

> The more aware you are of My Presence, the safer you feel. This is not some sort of escape from reality; it is tuning in to ultimate reality.

Dear Jesus,

You understand me wonderfully well! When I'm conscious of Your Presence, I feel safer and more peaceful. Sometimes, though, it's hard for me to remember You are still in charge of this world: especially when I watch the news on television. There is so much spin on what they present as fact, and You are invariably left out of the picture. It's a huge challenge to stay aware of You while media are bombarding me with evil and cynicism.

Beloved, one of the problems with television is that it puts viewers into a passive mode. If you come across something disturbing while you are reading, you can stop for a while and think about the matter. You can also take time to talk it over with Me. Television, however, sends a constant barrage of stimuli your way, making it hard for you to think about what you're seeing and hearing. Nonetheless, there are still some measures you can take to stay engaged with Me. You can pray before you even turn the set on, asking Me to help you view things from My perspective. When you have finished watching whatever you planned to see, take time to talk with Me about it. I will help you regain a biblical worldview.

I am indeed in charge of the world: I created it, and I sustain it. When you are aware of My Presence, you feel more at home in your surroundings. I am your ultimate dwelling place, and I am preparing a home for you in heaven. I am also continually with you on earth. Though you cannot see Me, the reality is that I am your home—both now on earth and forevermore in paradise.

Lord, you have been our dwelling place throughout all generations.
Before the mountains were born or you brought forth the earth
and the world, from everlasting to everlasting you are God.
Psalm 90:1–2

In my Father's house are many rooms; if it were not so, I would
have told you. I am going there to prepare a place for you.
John 14:2

Surely or only goodness, mercy and unfailing love shall follow
me all the days of my life, and through the length of my days the
house of the Lord [and His presence] shall be my dwelling place.
Psalm 23:6 AMP

There is no condemnation in My Presence,
for I view you robed in My righteousness.
Savor the delightfulness of your
guilt-free existence in Me.

Dear Jesus,

I am so thankful for Your robe of righteousness! The longer I know You, the more conscious I am of my utter unrighteousness. I could easily fall prey to self-hatred if I focused on all the ways I fall short. But I remind myself that You have clothed me with garments of salvation: setting me free from condemnation.

Beloved, I want to help you see yourself consistently the way I always view you: dazzling in royal righteousness. You may find it easier to see yourself this way when you are living up to your standard of performance. But you have never yet lived up to My standard, and you never will—in this life. You need My righteousness just as much on good days as on bad ones. A common pitfall is to think you can manage without Me when things are going well in your life.

At such times you may feel that you have no need of My royal robe. Another common pitfall is to become so preoccupied with your sinfulness and failures that you despair—forgetting that My salvation-clothing is sufficient to cover *all* your sins.

I want you to enjoy the riches of your salvation: the delightfulness of guilt-free existence in Me. I arrayed you in a robe of perfect righteousness when I became your Savior. Nothing and no one can strip you of that covering! The more consistently you see yourself clothed in My royal garments, the more you can rejoice in My radiant Presence. You are chosen royalty, belonging to Me—that you may proclaim My excellencies. I am the One who called you out of darkness into My marvelous Light!

> There is therefore now no condemnation for those who are in Christ Jesus. For the law of the Spirit of life in Christ Jesus has set you free from the law of sin and of death.
> *Romans 8:1–2 NASB*

> I delight greatly in the LORD; my soul rejoices in my God.
> For he has clothed me with garments of salvation
> and arrayed me in a robe of righteousness.
> *Isaiah 61:10*

> But you are a chosen race, a royal priesthood, a holy nation, a people for God's own possession, that you may proclaim the excellencies of Him who has called you out of darkness into His marvelous light.
> *1 Peter 2:9 NASB*

You can feel secure, even in the midst of cataclysmic changes, through awareness of My continual Presence. The One who never leaves you is the One who never changes. I am the same yesterday, today, and forever.

Dear Jesus,

I think what You are saying is: Because You never change, I have a firm foundation for handling whatever changes come my way. You are that foundation— the Rock on which I can build my life. However, catastrophes tend to destroy what people have built. I don't think I'm ready to face cataclysmic changes yet.

Beloved, I am indeed the firm foundation on which you can build your life. The significance of your life is not in buildings or other things that can be swept away by catastrophes. Though I want you to enjoy the material blessings I provide, you must not depend on them to feel safe. Real security rests in Me alone—not in Me plus favorable circumstances. If you build your life on the Rock of My Presence, nothing can destroy that

foundation: It is invincible! Moreover, the essence of
who you are—your soul—is indestructible.

You said you're not yet ready to face cataclysmic
change. I don't expect you to be ready for that until
the moment it actually occurs. But I am training you
to trust Me enough to believe you can handle anything
that happens—with My help. Remember My promise
that I will never leave you or forsake you. Though My
Presence with you is absolutely guaranteed, it reassures
you only to the extent that you are aware of Me. I am
vibrantly present in all your moments, but sometimes
you have to search for Me. Seek Me as a vital neces-
sity—not a luxury—and you will find Me; search for
Me with all your heart.

Jesus Christ is the same yesterday and today and forever.
Hebrews 13:8

Trust in the LORD forever, for the LORD, the LORD, is the Rock eternal.
Isaiah 26:4

"Never will I leave you; never will I forsake you."
Hebrews 13:5

Then you will seek Me, inquire for, and require Me [as a vital
necessity] and find Me when you search for Me with all your heart.
Jeremiah 29:13 AMP

I am a God of both intricate detail
and overflowing abundance. When you
entrust the details of your life to Me,
you are surprised by how thoroughly
I answer your petitions.

Dear Jesus,

I rejoice in Your overflowing abundance! Time after time I have come to You for Life, and You have provided plentifully. It amazes me that One so immeasurably great would care about the tiny details of my life.

Beloved, My infinite abundance enables Me to be attentive to every bit of your life. Actually, small matters can lead to major consequences, so it's wise to entrust to Me even things that seem unimportant. One way of doing this is through seeking to please Me in every aspect of your life. This changes your perspective and invites Me into all your moments. When you go through a day desiring to please Me, feelings of emptiness give way to abundant fullness. Things around you seem brighter, because the Light of My Presence casts a gentle glow on them. Your efforts to please Me draw us closer and put you in sync with My will. Thus connected with Me, you can enjoy sharing My pleasant, comfortable yoke and My light, easily borne burden.

You receive many blessings through entrusting the details of your life to Me. When you do so, I surprise you in several ways: I answer your prayers bountifully, and I awaken your heart to the radiant pleasure of living in union with Me.

The thief comes only to steal and kill and destroy;
I came that they may have life, and have it abundantly.
John 10:10 NASB

So we make it our goal to please him,
whether we are at home in the body or away from it.
2 Corinthians 5:9

You are my lamp, O LORD; the LORD turns my darkness into light.
2 Samuel 22:29

For My yoke is wholesome (useful, good—not harsh, hard,
sharp or pressing, but comfortable, gracious and pleasant),
and My burden is light and easy to be borne.
Matthew 11:30 AMP

Let Me fill you with My Love, Joy, and Peace; these are Glory-gifts, flowing from My living Presence. Though you are an earthen vessel, I designed you to be filled with heavenly contents.

Dear Jesus,

I am not only an earthen vessel, I am also a leaky container. I need to be filled and refilled—over and over again. Without You, my emptiness is profound. Please fill me with Your Love, Joy, and Peace in full measure.

Beloved, come to Me and linger in My Presence. I am eager to fill you with My Glory-gifts, but this takes time: focused time with Me. Do not rush into My Presence, trying to grab as much blessing as you can before making a quick exit. Instead, stay with Me a while, enjoying the awesome privilege of communing with your King. As you wait with Me, My very Life flows into you. I choose to fill you with heavenly substance, even though you are a jar of clay—and a leaky one at that!

I want you to be all Mine—filled to overflowing with My Love, Joy, and Peace. Because these Glory-gifts leak out of you, you need Me continually for renewal. Your neediness is not a mistake or defect: It keeps you looking to Me, depending on Me, communicating with Me. Though you are a frail earthen jar, I have filled you with the most precious treasure: the divine Light of the gospel. Your human frailty is necessary to show that this exceedingly great Power is not from you but from Me.

I am *Christ in you, the hope of Glory*. As I fill you with My Glory-gifts, let My wondrous Light shine through you into other people's lives.

But the fruit of the Spirit is love, joy, peace, patience...
Galatians 5:22

However, we possess this precious treasure [the divine Light of the Gospel] in [frail, human] vessels of earth, that the grandeur and exceeding greatness of the power may be shown to be from God and not from ourselves.
2 Corinthians 4:7 AMP

Christ in you, the hope of glory.
Colossians 1:27

In the same way, let your light shine before men, that they may see your good deeds and praise your Father in heaven.
Matthew 5:16

Topical Index

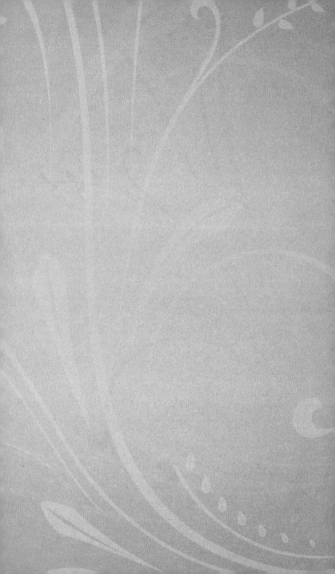